A MANUAL OF MARKS

ON

POTTERY AND PORCELAIN;

A DICTIONARY OF EASY REFERENCE.

BY

W. H. HOOPER AND W. C. PHILLIPS.

1876.

PREFACE.

This Manual, founded on the note-books of the Authors, was commenced some years ago, but was thrown aside on the announcement of other works which promised to supply the much wanted book of reference for the pocket.

It is now brought out, because a great number of Marks collected by the Authors have never yet been published—most of the Oriental being quite new—and their general arrangement will, it is hoped, make the book of great use to the collector.

Some of the European part has been derived from the works of Brongniart and Demmin. The Japanese part owes much of its value to the kindness and courtesy of Mr. A. G. Yamada, and the thanks of the Authors are also due to many gentlemen who have allowed their collections to be examined, and have given much valuable assistance.

Being only intended for a pocket-volume, unimportant factories and unknown marks are left out. For more detailed information, the works of Brongniart, Chaffers, Demmin, Jacquemart (admirably translated by Mrs. Bury Palliser), Marryat, Robinson and others may be consulted.

The work is divided into four parts; in the first, the Marks are classed under descriptive heads, as Anchor, Animal, etc.; in the second—Majolica—the factories of Italy are arranged alphabetically; in the third, other factories of Europe on the same plan; and in the fourth, the Oriental Marks are arranged by the number of characters inscribed.

The Marks on Pottery and Porcelain are of three kinds —factory, workman, and pattern mark. The first is usually placed in a prominent position, sometimes accompanied by the mark of the maker or decorator. Sevres Porcelain, for instance, often having four or five workmen's marks, besides that of the factory. The pattern mark is usually a number; this is seldom given, being useless without a description of the pattern itself.

The Marks when pencilled or incised, vary very considerably; a different hand, a full brush, or a flaw in the material, all tend to make them unrecognizable; even when printed they are often blurred by the action of the fire or running of the enamel, and when impressed, a shrinking of the wet clay will change or obliterate them.

CONTRACTIONS.

The quality of the Ware is described in the first column, and the mode of marking in the second, as follows :—

maj.	*Majolica.*	inc. ... ... *Incised.*
h. p.	*Hard Paste.*	imp. ... ... *Impressed.*
s. p.	*Soft Paste.*	p.... ... ... *Pencilled.*
pot.	*Pottery.*	pr. ... ... *Printed.*
		sten. ... ... *Stencilled.*

	ANCHOR.					
CHELSEA	...	...	...	s p	imp	174.
"	...	...	...	"	p gold or red	"
"	...	...	...	"	"	"
"	...	...	...	"	"	"
"	...	...	...	"	"	"
"	...	...	...	"	"	"
POPPLESDORF	...	...	...	pot	imp	176.
SCEAUX PENTHIEVRE	...	...	s p	p blue	175.

B

Sceaux Penthievre	pot	p blue	175.
Venice	h p	p red	1765
„ *This mark varies very much*	maj.	p color	17—
Cologne ... ·.. ...	pot	p blue	17—
Bow *The form and position of the sword vary.*	s p	p red	173-
Coalbrook Dale ...	h p	p blue	18—
Derby Chelsea ...	s p	p gold or red	1770

Mark	Place			
GM ⚓	**VENICE** ... ... *Giovanni Marconi*	s p	p gold or color	17—
⚓ **RH**	**WORCESTER** *Richard Holdship, decorator* *He also worked for Derby*		p color	175—
DAVENPORT ⚓	**LONGPORT**	pot	imp	1793
DAVENPORT STONE CHINA	"	"	pr blue	1805
LIVERPOOL ⚓	"	pot	imp	18—
MAFRA ⚓ CALDAS PORTUGAL	**CALDAS** *Imitation of Palissy Ware*	pot	imp	18—
MIDDLESBRO POTTERY ⚓ 20	**MIDDLESBOROUGH** ... 20, *Pattern mark*	pot	pr blue imp	"

ANIMAL.

SWINTON ... ... *The Rockingham Crest.*	h p	p red	1824
MEISSEN ... ... *Near Dresden.*	pot	imp	17—
HESSE CASSEL ...	h p	p blue	1763
AMSTERDAM	h p	p blue	1772
,, ...	,,	,,	,,
FRANKENTHAL ...	h p	p blue	1754
CHINA ... ... *On old Nankin Ware.*	h p	p blue	
,,	,,	,,	

ARROW.

Bow	...	...	...	s p	p blue	173–
(?) PLYMOUTH	...	...		h p	,,	,,
CAUGHLEY	...	..		b p	p blue	17—
LEEDS ...	...	...		pot	imp	177.

Also with name Hartley, Green & Co.

PARIS ...	...	...		h p	p blue	1773

De la Courtille (sometimes called Torches)

,,	...	...		,,	,,	,,

AXE.

BADEN BADEN				h p	p gold	
Widow Sperl.					or color	1753
,,	...	...		,,	,,	,,

BADEN BADEN *Widow Sperl.*	h p	p gold or color	1753
DELFT *De Byl (The Axe)* *Justus Brouwer*	pot	p blue	1764
,,	,,	,,	,,
,,	,,	,,	,,

BEACON.

GENOA	maj.	p	15—

BELL.

DELFT *De drei Klokken.* (The 3 bells) *W. Van der Does*	pot	p blue	1764
,, This *mark varies so much that it is called Leaf and Arrow head.*	,,	,,	,,
,,	,,	,,	,,

BIRD.

AMSTERDAM ...	pot	p color	1780
Hartog and Brandeis.			

ANSPACH	h p	p blue	1718
Sometimes used without the letter			

„	„	„	„

SÈVRES	h p	p red	1810
1st Empire.		sten &	
		imp	

Napoleon III. Emperor	h p	pr color	1852

LIVERPOOL	pot	p color	1833
A Liver, the Arms of the Town.			
Case, Mort & Co.			

Hague (The) *The Arms of.*		h p	p blue	177–
„ ...		„	„	„

BOW.

Bow		s p	p blue	173–

BUTTERFLY.

Chinese *On old Nankin*	h p	p blue	

CADUCEUS.

Dresden ... *This mark varies very much.*		h p	p blue	1712
Worcester ... *In imitation of Dresden*		s p	p blue	1753

CIRCULAR MARKS.

Faenza ... *And other varieties, and also without the circle*		maj.	p blue	15—
„ B.		„	„	„

Hœchst ... ... *The arms of the Archbishop of Mayence.*	h p	p gold or color	1720
„ *Dahl*	pot & h p	p color	1794
Damm *Aschafenberg*	h p	p blue	17—
Delft ... ... *T' Fortuyn* Fortune *P. Van der Breil*	pot	p blue	1691
„ *Martinus Gouda*	pot	„	1675
Florence ... ... *The arms of the Medici. Francis II. A very rare mark.*	s p	p color	15—
Urbino ... ... *Orazio Fontana Urbino fecit.*	maj.	p color	15—

DERBY	...	...	h p	pr color	1815
COLOGNE	...	...	pot		16—
MONTPELLIER *Le Vouland.*		...	pot	imp	18—
SHELTON	...	...	pot	pr color	1820
BERLIN *Royal Factory*	...	...	h p	pr	1850
SEVRES	...	...	h p	pr color	1830

The mark was used with the year date from 1830.

Louis Philippe	h p	,,	1834

SEVRES		h p	pr color	1834
„ *Republic*		h p	p red	1848
BURSLEM ... *Wedgwood & Bentley*		pot & h p	imp	1768

CLAW.

DELFT *De Klaauw* (The Claw) *Lambertus Sanderus.*		pot	p blue	1764
„		„	„	„
„		„	„	„
„		„	„	„

CRESCENT.

SALOPIAN.	CAUGHLEY ... *And without name.*	h p.	p blue	1750
	WORCESTER ...	s p	p blue or gold	1751
	„	„	„	„
	URBINO ... *Also with the initials E. F. B.*	maj.	p blue	1594
	NAPLES ...	maj.	p blue	17—
Flight	WORCESTER ...	h p	p blue	1783

MARIEBERG, Sweden	pot & **s p**	p color	1750
Ehrenreich,	„	„	1759

—

CROSS.

BRISTOL ...	h p	p in color	1773
FULDA ..	h p	p blue	1763
VARAGES ...	pot	p bh o'r or red	1730
DRESDEN ..	h p	p blue	1720
COPENHAGEN	h p	p color	1772
CASEMENE ...	pot	imp	18—

Bourg-la-Reine *Le Chappelet.*	h p	p	17—
Bristol ...	h p	p color	1773
Turin *Vineuf* *Dr. Gioanetti.*	h p	imp	1770

CROWN.

Bassano *Also with the signature of Antonio Terchi & Bo Terchj*	maj.	p color	1540
Castelli ...	maj.	p color	16—
St. Petersburg *Alexander I.*	h p	p blue or color	1801
Alexander II.	h p	p blue or color	1865

PARIS *Porcelaine de la Reine (Antoinette)*	h p	p red	1778
VENICE ...	maj	17—
DERBY ...	s p	p gold	177-
BRUSSELS ...	h p	p color	18—
WORCESTER ... *Barr, Flight & Barr.*	h p	imp	1807
NAPLES ... *Crown of various shapes.* *sometimes B.C.*	maj.	p	16—
SEVRES *Charles X.*	h p	p blue	1829

SEVRES *Charles X.*	h p	p blue	1829
LUDWIGSBURG *Also attributed to*	...	h p	p blue	1758
BUEN RETIRO *Madrid. Carlos III.*	...	s p & pot	p color	176–
LUDWIGSBURG *Initial of Duke Charles*	...	h p	p blue	1758
NIEDERVILLER *De Custine, director*	...	h p & pot	p blue	1786
„	...	„	„
URBINO (?) *Luca Cambiasi*	...	maj.	„	16–
HOCHST	...	h p	p gold & color	1720

PARIS			h p	p blue	1769
Charles Philippe, Comte d'Artois, patron					
FRANKENTHAL			h p	p blue	1761
Carl Theodore					
DERBY			h p	p red or violet	1780
Duesbury					
„ *with monogram* D K *Duesbury and Kean* ...			„	„	1798
„ *also without crown* ...			„	„	„
„ *Stevenson & Hancock* ...			„	„	186–
HILDERSHEIM			h p	p blue	1760

Fulda ...	...	...	h p	p blue	1763
Capo di Monti, Naples	...	s p	p color	1780	
Ferdinandus Rex					
Paris ...	...	...	h p	p red	1780
Dihl and Guerhard					
Hesse Darmstadt	...	h p	p blue	1756	
St. Petersburg ...	...	h p	p color	1825	
Nicholas I.					
Sèvres	...	...	h p	imp or pr color	1845
Louis-Philippe					
Clignancourt ...	...	h p	st red	1780	

Buen Retiro, Madrid	...	s p	p color	176-
Marieberg, Sweden	...	pot & s p	p color	1750
„	...	...	„	„	„
Capo di Monti, Naples	...	s p	p red or blue	1759
„	...	...	„	„ & imp	„
Sèvres. *Napoleon III.* *In this year the manufacture of soft paste was resumed*	...	s & h p	p color	1854
Savona. (?) *Guidobono*	...	maj.	„	16—
Orléans	...	...	pot	p color	1753

St. Petersburg. *Paul I.* ...	h p	p color	1796
Dresden ... ... *Sachsiche Porzellen Manufacture*	h p	p blue	1750
Ludwigsburg	h p	p blue	1806
Oporto ... ... *Vista Allegra*	h p	p gold or color	1790
Worcester ... ... *Flight and Barr*	h p	p color	1793
Liverpool	pot	imp & pr color	1796

DOME.

Florence ... ... *A rare mark*	s p	p color	1580

'DOT.				
LIMBACH ...	...	h p	p	1761
URBINO & FAENZA	...	maj.	p	16—
ERMINE.				
STOKE-ON-TRENT ...	...	h p	p color & gold	185-
Minton				
FISH.				
GENOA ...	...	maj.	p	16—
NYON ...	...	h p	p blue	1790
LILLE ...	...	h p	sten & p red	1784
The Dauphin. Patron				
CHINA ...	...	h p	p blue	969 to 1106
Old Nankin ware				
This mark varies much				

China ...	...	...	h p	p blue	969 to 1106
" ...	...	...	"	"	"

FLEUR-DE-LYS.

Bow ...	...	...	s p	p blue	173–
Capo di Monti, Naples	...	s p	p blue	1736
Removed to Buen Retiro, Madrid	...	"	"	176–
Marseilles ...	...	pot	pr color	1777
"			"	p "	"
Rouen ...	...	...	"	p color	1542
" ...	...	...	"	"	℀.

St. Cloud	...	...	s p	imp	1702
Sèvres		...	h p	p blue	1830

FLOWER.

China.	(?) *Sesamum*	...	h p	p color	1403 to 1424
„	...	...	...	„	p red & gold	1426 to 1435
„	...	...	...	„	„	„
„	(?) *Emblems of longevity* These marks are from old Nankin ware; date uncertain			„	p blue	
„	...	...	...	„	„	
„	...	...	...	„	„	

CHINA ...	...	...	h p	p blue
„	...	...	„	„
„	...	...	„	„
„	...	...	„	„
JAPAN. *On old and modern ware in imitation of old Nankin patterns*		...	h p	„
„	...	...	„	„
„	...	...	„	„

GRASS.

CHINA. *This mark is known as the " Grass Mark," but it is meant for a water plant* ...   h p   p blue   960 to 963

,, ...   ,,   ,,   ,,

,, ...   ,,   ,,   ,,

,, ...   ,,   ,,   ,,

———

HAYFORK.

RUDOLSTADT   ...   ...   h p   p color   1758

,, ...   ,,   p blue   ,,

,, ...   ,,   ,,   17—
Also WORCESTER

HATCHET (*see* AXE).

————

HEAD.

DELFT ...   .   pot   p color

————

HEART.

MOUSTIERS. *Olery*   ...   pot   p color   17—

NAPLES   ...   ...   maj   „   15—

ST. SAMSON   ...   ...   pot   imp   183–

————

HORN.

CHANTILLY   ...   ...   s p   p blue   1725
                                  or imp

LUDWIGSBURG ...   ...   h p   p red or   1758
                                  blue

LABEL.

ORLEANS ...	...	h &	p color	1753
Gerault Daraubert		s p		

LEAF.

BERLIN
*This mark is frequently painted
in green or gold over the Berlin
sceptre on damaged pieces*

GROSBREITENBACH	...	h p	p color	1770
„ *Sometimes a mere flourish*		„	„	„
CHINA ...	... ...	h p	p blue	

*A great variety of leaves are
found on old Nankin ware,
the mark was imitated by
DELFT and other factories*

„	...	...	„	„
„	...	...	„	„
„	...	...	„	„
„	...	...	:"	„
„	...	...	„	„

CHINA.

(?) Bamboo leaves, mark of a Factory in King-te-chin ...	h p	p blue	1573 1619
„ ... ... „		„	„

JAPAN. *On ware painted with Chinese patterns*   h p   p blue

LETTERS.

PARIS. *Le bœuf* ...   ...   „   p red   177-
A is also found on BOW *ware*

ANSPACH. *This mark varies very much and sometimes looks like crossed swords* ...   h p   p blue   1718

DELFT ... ... *De Griekse A* (The Alpha) *J. T. Dickstraat or Dextra*				pot	p blue	1764
„				„	„	„
DELFT ... ... *De Witte Ster* (The White Star) *A Kiell*				pot	p blue	„
„				„	„	„
ALTENROLHAU ... ... *A Nowotny Director*				h p & pot	imp	1829
URBINO ... ... *Alphonso Patanazzi*				maj	p	160–
ARRAS				s p	p blue	1782
DELFT				pot	p	17—

WORCESTER	h p	mo	1793
Barr. B is also on Bow ware			
MARSEILLES	pot	p color	1769
Bonnefoy			
DELFT	pot	p blue	175—
I. Brouwer			
SAINTES	pot	inc	1538
Attributed to Bernard Pallissy			
BRISTOL	h p	p color	1773
GUBBIO	maj	p color	15—
Maestro Giorgio			
LUXEMBOURG	pot	p color	1806
Boch	& h p		
BOURG LA REINE ...	s p	p blue	1773
	& pot		
DELFT	pot	p blue	

BP	BAYREUTH	pot	p blue	15—
Bt	DELFT ... ... (?) *Berghem*	pot	p blue	
BVDD	DELFT ... ... (?) *Van der Does*	pot	p blue	
C c	ST. PETERSBURG ... ... *Catherine*	h p	„	176—
CB	BAYREUTH	h p	p color	1744
CB DRW	DELFT — ... ... De Paauw (The Peacock) (?) *Cornelis Boumeester*	pot	p blue	17—
C.D.	COALBROOK DALE ...	h p	p blue	1787
C·D	LIMOGES	h p	p red	1773
C.H	PARIS ... ... *Chanou*	h p	„	1784

Mark	Name			Type	Process	Date
+C+ +S+	SINCENY Joseph le Cerf	...	...	pot	p color	177-
D	DERBY ... Duesbury	...	...	s p	p red	1756
D	CAUGHLEY (*A Crescent, not a Letter, though often mistaken for one*)			h p	p blue	1750
D2	LILLE ... Dorez	...	...	pot	p color	174-
ꝑD	ROUEN	...	...	pot	p color	15—
DEX	DELFT ... (*de Griekse A*) (The Alpha) T. *Dextra*	...	...	pot	p blue	1764
D.S.K / 1	DELFT ... (*de Dubbelde Schenkkan*) (The Double Can)	...	...	pot	p blue	,,
D V	MENECY VILLEROY Duc de Villeroy, patron	...	s p	p color & inc	1735
ℰℭ	ST. PETERSBURG ... Catherine II.	...	h p	p blue	1762

ᑕᑭᴋ	Sᴛ. Pᴇᴛᴇʀsʙᴜʀɢ ... ... *P. Korniloffe*		h p	p blue	1762
ЖЕ	Mᴀʀɪᴇʙᴇʀɢ ... ... *Ehrenreich, director*		pot & s p	p color	1759
E B S	Dᴇʟғᴛ ... ... *T" jongue Moriaans Hofft* (The young Moors head.)		pot	p	1764
Ŧ	Bʀɪsᴛᴏʟ ... ... (*Imitation Oriental.*)		h p	p color	1773
F	Fʟᴏʀᴇɴᴄᴇ ... ... (*A late mark on Fine Pottery.*)		maj	„	17—
Ŧ ℱ	Fᴀᴇɴᴢᴀ ... ... (*Many varieties of the letter* *are found.*)		maj	„	14—
ℱ	Fᴜʀsᴛᴇɴʙᴇʀɢ		h p	p blue	1750
Ƒ	„ ... ... *F is also found on Bow ware*		„		„
Ƒ/180	Dᴇʟғᴛ		pot	p blue	

c

𝓕꞉꞉𝓧꞉ Rou:	URBINO. *F꞊ᵒ Xanto* ...	maj.	p color	15—
F^d fd	MOUSTIERS. *Féraud* ...	pot	p color	178–
F.D.V N	NAPLES ... ... *Fab. del Vecchio, Napoli*	maj. & h p	imp	17--
FI	FLORENCE. *For Firense* ...	maj.	p	17—
F.P. 1617	URBINO. *F꞊ᵒ Patanassi* ...	maj.	p	1608
F.R	NEVERS	pot	p color	1730
F&R	PERKENHAMMER. *Fischer & Reichembach*	h p	„	1802
T↑R ⋀⋀ 1536	GUBBIO	maj.	„	1536
G	CAFFAGIOLO. *G is found on Bow ware*	„	„	1507

𝒢	NAPLES. *Giustiniani*	...	maj.	imp & p color	17—
𝒢𝒢	GERA ...	...	...	h p	p blue	1780
𝒢 𝒢	GOTHA ...	...	...	„	„	175–
G·B·C	DELFT	...	...	pot	p red	
G꜔G ᵽᵽ9	„	...	...	„	p	17—
ᴄᴠᴘ	„ *T'oude Moriaans Hofft.* (The old Moor's head) *Geertruy Verstelle.*			pot	p blue	1764
.Ħ	STRASBOURG. *Hannong*	...	h p & pot	„	1752
H	PARIS. *Hannong*	...	„	p color	1773
✝H·B	NEVERS. *Henri Borne*	...	pot	p color	168–
Ḣ ⁊ 𝟕𝟏	DELFT. *Jacobus Halder Adriens zoon* ...	...	...	„	p color	1765

H . F	Naples	...	...	maj.	p	17—
HS.J R	Delft ...	...	...	pot	p red	
HSK.VN	Nuremberg	...	...	pot	p blue	15—
	Hans Kraut Villingen					
HVH	Delft ...	...	...	pot	p blue	1764
	Hendrick Van Hoorn					
HVMD	Delft ...	...	...	pot	p blue	„
	T'Hart (The Hart)	...				
	Hendrick van Middeldijk					
IAG	Lisbon	...	...	pot	imp	18—
IDM	Delft ...	...	...	pot	p blue	1764
	(?) *Jacobus de Milde*					
JKF 1132	Delft ...	...	...	pot	p blue	

IⵄK	DELFT ... ... *Jan Kuylich*			pot	p blue	1680
I.P	(?) PESARO. (?) In Pesaro	...		maj	p	
ITD / 7	DELFT ... ... *De Griekse A* (The Alpha) *J. T. Dikstraat or Dextra.*			pot	p blue	1764
ⵏW	DELFT ...	...	...	,,	,,	
J.J.8	DELFT ...	...	...	,,	,,	
jP.	PARIS ... ... *Jacob Petit*			h p .	p blue	1790
J.P / L	LIMOGES ... ... *J. Pouyat*			pot	p red	18—
JZ	VOISONLIEU ... ... *Jean Zeigler*			pot	at color & imp	1839
K	DELFT ... ... (?) *Jan Kuylich*			pot	p blue	

DELFT ... ... *Jan Kuylich*			pot	p blue	1680	
KIEL ... ... *Buchwald, director* *A. Leihamer, decorator*			,,	p gold or color	177 -	
DRESDEN			h p	p blue	17—	
,, ...			,,	,,	,,	
DELFT			pot	,,	17—	
LIMBACH			h p	p red	1761	
MONTELUPO ... ... Given by Jacquemart, *Wolfs Brush*			maj.	p		
BRUSSELS ... ... *L. Cretté*			h p	p color	1791	
DELFT ... ... *De Lampetkan* (The Pitcher) *Widow G. Brouwer*			pot	p blue	1764	

℞	BORDEAUX ... ... *Lahens and Rateau*	h p	p color	18—
L ♭	DELFT ... ... (?) *Van Dammelar*	pot	p blue	
-M-	CAFFAGIOLO	maj	p	15—
M	SINCENY ... ... *Moulin*	pot	p color	1864
MAP	PARIS ... ... *Morel à Paris*	h p	p blue	1773
.M.ᵩ	GUBBIO ... ... *Maestro Giorgio*	maj		15—
	„	„	„	„
1572				
M ჟ	„	„	„	„
M:o·L	LOOSDRECHT ... ... *Manufactur oude Loosdrecht* *Moll director*	h p	p blue	1772

M.P	OPORTO ... ... pot	p gold or color	17—
	Rocha Soare		
MP	DELFT ... ... pot	p blue	1639
	De Metaale Pot (The Metal Pot)		
	Lambertus Cleffius		
MVC / 4	DELFT ... ... pot	„	
N	NEVERS ... ... pot	p color	15—
1322	GUBBIO ... ... maj	p	153·
N	*Vincentio or Cencio son of*		
	Maestro Giorgio		
			•
1335 N	GUBBIO ... ... „	„	„
OP.	BOURG-LA-REINE ... ... h p	p blue	1773
₽	LILLE ... ... pot	p color	1778
	Petit		

P P	LIVERPOOL		pot	p gold	1760
	Pennington		& h p	or color	
				& imp	
P P	PINXTON		s p	p color	1791
	These letters are ascribed to Pinxton, but the ware was seldom marked				
P	GUBBIO		maj	p	15—
	? Maestro Perestino				
P/15	DELFT		pot	p	
PA	CAFFAGIOLO		maj	p	15—
PA	ROUEN		pot	p color	15—
PBC	NIMES		"	imp	183.
	Plantier, Boncourant & Co.				
PP	ROUEN		pot	p color	15—
P.D	DELFT		pot	p blue	1764
	P v Doorne				

PVDB	DELFT	pot	p blue	1691
	P van der Breil			
PVM	DELFT	pot	p blue	1764
	P van Meerum			
ℛ	DELFT	„	p brown	
Ṙ	MARSEILLES	pot & h p	p black	1777
	Robert			
R	REGENSBERG OR RATISBON	h p	p blue	17—
R-g	„ „ ...	h p	p blue	17—
R—n	RAUENSTEIN	h p	p blue	1760
R.S	DELFT	pot	„	
RVH	COLOGNE	pot	p blue	16—

S	CAUGHLEY *Salopian*	... '	...	h p	p blue	1750
S	SCHLAKENWALD	...	...	h p	p color	180\
·S·	SINCENY	...	...	pot	p color	1733
S.48	SEVRES *on white ware*		...	h p	pr green	1833
S/61	" *The Scratch denotes that the piece left the factory undecorated.*			"	"	186-
S:C T	ST. CLOUD *Trou Director*	...	...	pot & s p	p blue	173–
S X	SCEAUX PENTHIEVRE		...	s p	inc	1750
Ven⁝	VENICE	...	...	maj & h p	p color	15— 17—
W	BERLIN *Wegeley, founder*	...	...	h p	p blue	1751

W	PLYMOUTH ..: ... *Probably the usual mark, the sign Jupiter, carelessly pencilled*	h p	p blue	176-
WW	WORCESTER	s p	p blue	1751
	" ... ... *And others in imitation of oriental marks*	"	"	"
W.VB	DELFT ... ... *De Twee Wildemans* (The two Savages) *Willem Van Beek*	pot	p blue	1764
W.V.D.B	DELFT ... ... *Widow van der Briel*	pot	p blue	1764
1539	URBINO ... ... *F^co Xanto*	maj	p	15—
X.N	"	maj	X p blue N red lustre	,
X Z A	"	maj	p	"

Gubbio	...	...	maj	p	15—
Zurich	...	...	h p	p blue	1759
Delft ... *Dextra zoon*	...	...	pot	p	1765

LINES.

Alt Haldensteben	...	h p	imp	17—
Copenhagen *The Sound, the great and little Belts*	...	...	h p	p blue	1772
St. Petersburg	...	h p	p blue	17—
„	...	„	„	„

MITRE.

Wurzburg	...	...	h p	p blue	17—

MONOGRAMS.

ÆB	LILLE ...	...	...	pot	p color	17—
ℬ𝒜	AMSTERDAM or Amstel	...		h p	p blue	178-
	Daeuber director					
𝒜𝒟	PARIS ...	...	...	h p	p color	1773
	Gros Caillou Advenir Lamarre					
ADB ANNO 1774	DELFT ...	...	...	pot	p blue	1774
ADW	ANDENNES	...	...	pot	imp	18—
	A Der Vander Wœrt					
A	MOSCOW	...	...	h p	p color	17 —
	A Gardner					
AGA	GUBBIO	...	...	maj	p	1519
	Giorgio Andreoli					1537
AK AK	DELFT ...	...	...	pot	p blue	1764
	De witte Ster (The White Star)					
	A Kielle					

DELFT ... ... A *Kielle*			pot	p blue	1764
„			„	„	„
„			„	„	„
MOSCOW ... ... A *Popoff*			h p	p color	1830
APREY			pot	p black	1750
„			„	„	„
DELFT ... ... De *twee Scheepjes* (The two Ships) *Ant Pennis*			pot	p blue	1764
MOSCOW ... ... A *Popoff*			h p	p color	1830
DELFT ... ... *Keyser & Pynaker*			pot	p blue	1680
„			„	„	„

DELFT ... ... *Keyser & Pynaker*			pot	p color	1680
,, ...			,,	,,	,,
DRESDEN ... ... *Augustus Rex*			h p	p blue	1709
DRESDEN ... ... *A modern mark*			,,	p blue & imp	18—
PARIS ... ... *Reverend*			pot	p blue	16—
DELFT			,,	,,	16—
ANSPACH or Frankenthal ... *J. A. Hannong*			h p	,,	17—
TOURS ... ... *Victor Avisseau*			h p	,,	184-
NEVERS ... ... *Jacques Bourdu*			pot	p color	1602

LUXEMBOURG ... ... *Boch*	pot & h p	p color	1806
NIEDERVILLER ... ... *Beyerlé founder*	h p & pot	p blue	1760
MARANS ... ... *Jean Pierre Roussencq*	pot	p color	1740
NYON ... ... *Pierre Mülhausen decorator*	h p	p blue	18—
COALBROOK DALE ...	h p	p blue	1787
URBINO ... ... *A similar mark is dated 1549.*	maj	p	15—
STOKE-ON-TRENT ...	h p	pr color	185-
SEVRES ... ... *Charles X.*	h p	p blue	1824

Venice ... ... *Probably Gian Andrea and Pietro Bertolini*	maj	p			15—
Coalbrook Dale ...	h p	p blue			1787
Diruta	maj	p			16—
Paris ... ... *Chanou*	h p	p red			1784
Urbino ... ... *Nicolo d' Urbino*	maj	p			15—
Delft ... ... *De Paauw (The Peacock) Jacobus de Milde 1764*	pot	p blue			1651
,, ...	,,	,,			,,
,, ...	,,	,,			,,

ДҪ	DIRUTA	...	...	maj	p	16—
DL.1429 FAC-ERAT	FLORENCE	...	...	maj	p	14—
DF	NEVERS Denis Lefebvre	...	...	pot	p color	1636
EX	DELFT ... Johannes Mesch	...	...	pot	p blue	1680
Æ	URBINO	...	...	maj	,,	16—
A	TOULOUSE Fouqué Arnoux & Co.	...	...	pot	p color	1820
B B	LILLE ... F. Boussemart	...	...	pot	p color	1729
F	KREUSSEN Caspar Vest Hans Christophe Vest	...	...	pot	p color	1610 1690
R	PARIS ... Dihl & Guerhard, Duc d'Angouléme patron	...	...	h p	p red	1780

CL	NUREMBERG ... ... *George Liebolt*	pot	p blue	1667
HB	DELFT ... . *De drei porceleyne Fleschjes* (The 3 porcelain bottles) *Hugo Brouwer*	pot	p blue	1764
KD **1550**	NUREMBERG	pot	imp	1550
HF	NAPLES	maj	p	17—
HK	DELFT ... ... *Jan Jan zoon Kuylich*	pot	p blue	1680
HK	„	„	„	„
HK	NUREMBERG ... ... *Hans Kraut*	pot	p blue	15—
PH	STRASBOURG & FRANKENTHAL *Paul Hannong*	pot & h p	p blue & inc	17—

	GUBBIO ... ... *Hipollito Rombariotti*	maj	p	16—
	STRASBOURG & FRANKENTHAL *Hannong*	pot & h p	p blue	17—
	FRANKENTHAL & STRASBOURG *J. & P. Hannong*	,,	,,	,,
	NEVERS ... ... *Jacques Seigne*	pot	p color	17—
	NIEDERVILLER ... *Lanfray*	pot & h p	sten	1802
	LIMBACH (?)	h p	p color	176-
	,,	,,	p gold	,,
	PARIS ... ... *Gros Caillou*	h p	p color	1773

SEVRES	...	...	s p	p blue	1753
The letter indicates the date *See Sévres*					
"	...	...	h p	p blue	1814
Louis XVIII.					
MOUSTIERS *Olery*		...	pot	p color	17—
REGENSBERG or Ratisbon		...	h p	p blue	17—
COLOGNE	...	...	pot	p blue	1589
HEREND	...	...	h p	p blue	1839
Maurice Fischer					
DELFT ...	...	...	pot	p blue	1639
De Metaale Pot (The Metal Pot)					

	FAENZA	...	...	maj	p	154—
	„	...	...	„	„	„
	„	...	...	„	-	„
	URBINO	...	...	maj	p	15—
	Nicolo d' Urbino					
	DELFT ...	...	...	pot	p blue	1680
	Q Kleynoven					
	URBINO	...	...	maj	p	15—
	Orasio Fontana					
	CLIGNANCOURT	...	...	h p	st red	1775
	Monogram of the patron Louis Stanislas Xavier Comte de Provence					
	DELFT ...	...	...	pot	p	16—
	(?) Philip Wouvermans					

	DELFT		pot	p blue	1680
	J. Pynaker, C. Keyser & A. Pynaker				
	DELFT		pot	p blue	1764
	De Romeyn (The Roman) *Petrus van Meerum*				
	DELFT		pot	„	1691
	P van der Briel				
	DELFT		pot	p blue	1764
	De porceleyne Fles (The porcelain bottle) *Pieter van Doorne*				
	SEVRES		h & s p	p color	1792
	République Française				
	GUBBIO		maj	p	16—
	(?) *Salimbene*				
	COALBROOK DALE ...		h p	p blue	1861
	Caughley Swansea & Nantgarw				

ℛ	DELFT ... ... *Samuel Piet Roerder*			pot	p blue	165—
	DIRUTA			maj	p	16—
	CAFFAGGIOLO			maj	p	15—
	,, ...			,,	,,	,,
	ST. AMAND ... ... *Fauquez*			pot	p	175.
	STOKE-ON-TRENT ... *Minton*			h p	p blue or red	179-
	CASTELLI ... ... *Saverio Grue*			maj	p	17—
	DELFT ... ... *Suter van der Even*			pot	p blue	1580

SCHAFFHAUSEN ... *Tobias Stimmer*	...	...	pot	p color	1560
FAENZA	...	...	maj	p	15—
DELFT ... *Antoni Ter Humpelin*	...	...	pot	p blue	1650
NEVERS *Tite Ristori*	...	...	pot	p color	1850
DELFT *Jan van der Kloot Jan Zoon*	...	...	pot	p blue	1764
DELFT (?) *Van der Even*	...	...	pot	p blue	1580
„	...	...	„	„	„
„	...	...	„	„	„
PESARO (?) *Giovanni Vejaso*	...	...	maj	p	15—
MARSEILLES *Veuve Perrin*	...	...	pot	p black	1760

℟	Urbino	...	...	maj	p blue	16—
ᏔᎠ	Delft ... (?) *W van der Does*	...	...	pot	p blue	1764

MUSICAL INSTRUMENTS.

China ... *Nankin ware*	...	...	h p	p blue	

NAMES.

W- Adams.	Tunstall	...	...	pot	imp	1780
Astbury.	Shelton	...	...	pot	imp	17—
R. & J. Baddeley,	„	...	...	pot	imp	1750
Bailey & Batkin.	Lane End	...	...	pot	imp	18—
Baldasara manara	Faenza	...	...	maj	p	15—
Barr, Flight & Barr.	Worcester	...	...	h p	pr	1807

Enoch Booth.	TUNSTALL	...	pot	imp		1750
Brameld.	SWINTON ...	...	b p & pot	pr red		1807
ЛН *Verboom* ХБоот	DELFT ... *Verboom painter*	...	pot	p color		1680
ВРАТЬЕВЪ КОРНИЛОВЫХЪ	ST. PETERSBURG ... *Korneloffski Brothers*	...	h p	pr color		1827
CAMBRIAN	SWANSEA ...	...	h p	p color		178–
Richard Chaffers	LIVERPOOL ...	...	pot	p color		1751
Chamberlain.	WORCESTER ...	...	h p	p color & imp		178–
Child.	TUNSTALL	...	pot	imp		1763
Christian.	LIVERPOOL	...	pot	imp		1765
Coalport.	COALBROOK DALE ...	...	h p	p blue		1787

Copeland.	STOKE-ON-TRENT ...	...	h p & pot	imp	1847	
	Copeland and Garrett, 1833					
	Copeland, late Spode, 1847					
Dagoty.	PARIS ...	...	...	h p	p red	179–
Davenport.	LONGPORT	...	...	pot	imp	1793
Dihl.	PARIS...	...	...	h p	p red	1780
DON GIORGIO 1489	FAENZA (?)	...	...	maj	p	1489
Duÿn	DELFT ...	...	...	pot	p blue	1764
	De porceleyne Schootel (The porcelain plate)					
	J. van Duÿn					
Eastwood.	HANLEY	...	...	pot	imp	179–
Elers.	BRADWELL	...	...	pot	imp	1690
Feuillet.	PARIS ...	...	...	h p	p red	179–

Flight.	WORCESTER	...	...	h p	p color	1783
Flight & Barr	„ ...	...	...	„	„	1793
Flight, Barr & Barr.	„ ...	...	...	„	„	1807
⁴⁄₅𝘍𝘰𝘳𝘵𝘶𝘺𝘯	DELFT ...	...	pot	p blue	1691
	T. Fortuyn (Fortune)					
	P van der Breil					
ФГ ГУЛИНА	MOSCOW	...	...	h p & pot	imp color	18—
	Galena. Fabrica Gospodina					
	The Factory of our Lady)					
ГАРЛНЕРЪ	MOSCOW	...	...	h p	imp	17—
	Gardner					
Ginori.	DOCCIA	...	...	s p	imp	1735
Giustiniani IⓥN	NAPLES	...	...	maj	imp	17—
	Giustiniani Brothers					
Grainger, Lee & Co.	WORCESTER	...	...	h p	p red	1800
GRATAPAGLI FE:TAVR	TURIN (so attributed)	...	maj	p	17—
Guerhard et Dihl.	PARIS ...	...	...	h p	st red	1780

Hackwood.	SHELTON	...	...	pot	imp	1842
Harley.	LANE END	...	...	pot & h p	imp	1809
Heath.	DERBY ...	...	...	pot	imp	1760
Herculaneum.	LIVERPOOL	...	...	„	imp	1796
T. & J.Hollins.	SHELTON	...	...	pot	imp	18—
Housel.	PARIS ... "*De la reine*"	...	...	h p	p color	1799
A.& E.Keeling.	TUNSTALL	...	...	pot	imp	1770
KiEBb **15**	KIEF ...	...	...	pot	p color	178–
Hans Knaut *1578*	NUREMBERG	...	...	pot	p color	1578
Lakin & Poole.	HANLEY	...	...	pot	imp	177–
J. Lockett.	LANE END	...	...	pot	imp	17—
Mason's Ironstone China.	HANLEY, *Lane Delph near*	...	pot	pr color	1813

E. Mayer.	HANLEY	...	...	pot	imp	177–
Mayr & Newbd.	LANE END	...	...	pot	imp or pr color	18—
T. Mayer.	STOKE-ON-TRENT...		...	pot	imp	182–
Meigh.	HANLEY	...	...	pot	imp	178–
	STOKE-ON-TRENT ...		...	h p	pr	18—
Nast.	PARIS ...	...	...	h p	st red	1783
Neeld.	HANLEY	...	...	pot	imp	178–
Neale.	„	...	...	pot	imp	1776
Neale & Co.	„	...	...	„	„	1778
	DELFT ...	...	...	pot	p blue	1651
Pennington.	LIVERPOOL	...	...	h p & pot	imp & p color	1760
Phillips.	LONGPORT	...	...	pot	imp	„

Phillips & Co.	SUNDERLAND	...	...	pot	pr color	1780
B. Plant.	LANE END	...	...	pot	imp	177–
ПОПОВЫ	MOSCOW *A Popoff*	...	...	h p	p color	1830
Pouyat & *Russinger.*	PARIS ... *De la Courtille*	...	...	h p	p red	1773
Reid & Co.	LIVERPOOL	...	...	h p	imp	175–
Rockingham.	SWINTON	...	...	pot & h p	imp	1757
Sadler & Green.	LIVERPOOL	...	...	pot & h p	pr color	1756
William Sans.	BURSLEM	...	...	pot	imp	167–
MN^{le} Sèvres	SEVRES *National Factory*	...	...	s p	st red	1803
MImp^{le} de Sevres	,, *Imperial Factory*	...	...	h p	st red	1806

D

Sevres (mark)	SEVRES *Republic*	...	...	s p	p color	1792
Shaw.	LIVERPOOL	...	...	pot	imp	170–
R. Shawe.	BURSLEM	...	...	pot	imp	173–
Shorthose.	HANLEY	...	...	pot	imp	1770
Shorthose & Heath.	,,	...	...	pot	imp	18—
T. SNEYD.	,,	...	...	pot	imp	18—
SPODE.	STOKE-ON-TRENT	...	...	pot / h p	imp / p red	1770
Steel.	BURSLEM	...	...	pot	imp	18—
Steen (mark)	DELFT	...	...	pot	p	1650
THARI (mark)	,, ...	...	...	pot	p	1764
THOMAS TOFT (mark)	BURSLEM *Also Ralph Toft*	...	...	pot	in relief	1670
TURNER.	LANE END	...	...	pot	imp	1276

WyVelde	DELFT ...	...	...	pot	p		1660
1769 *S:Vizeer*	„ ...	...	...	pot	p		1769
Voyez.	COBRIDGE	...	...	pot	imp		1773
Aaron Wood.	BURSLEM	...	...	pot	imp		1750
Enoch Wood.	„	...	...	pot	imp		1783
Wood & Caldwell.	„	...	...	„	„		1790
WEDGWOOD.	„	...	⁄ ...	h p & pot	imp		175–
Wedgwood&Co	FERRYBRIDGE	...	...	h p & pot	imp		1796

NUMERAL.

	CAUGHLEY	...	...	h p	p blue	177-

There are many other numerals thus pencilled, to resemble Oriental marks

MALTA...	...	...	pot	imp	18—
NEVERS	...	...	pot	p color	15—
PLYMOUTH	...	...	h p	p blue	176–
This mark, the sign of Jupiter, is often considered as 2, 4 joined					
ST. CLOUD	...	...	pot	p color	1700
J. B. Chicanneau					
DELFT ...	...	...	pot	p	
ORB.					
BERLIN	...	...	h p	p blue	1830
SAVONA	...	...	maj	p	16—

Gubbio	maj	p	15—
ORIENTAL.			
China	h p	p blue	
Old Nankin ware. *Sacred axe*			
„ *Precious things.* Instruments of writing	„	„	
„ „ ...	„	„	
„ „ ...	„	„	
„ *Kwei,* or emblems of a Mandarin	„	„	
„ „ ...	„	„	
„ „ ...	„	„	
„ „ ...	„	„	

CHINA		h p	p blue		
Instrument used as a tuning fork					
DELFT		pot	p blue	18—	
In imitation of the 'six mark'					

OVAL.

ANDENNES		pot	imp	18—	
B. Lammens & Co.					
UZES		pot	imp	18—	
François Pichon					
(?) VENICE		maj	p	18—	
On modern ware					
MONTET		pot	mp	18—	
Laurjorois					
PESARO AND FAENZA ...		maj	p	15—	

	PESARO AND FAENZA	...	maj	p	15—
	VAL SOUS MENDON *Mittenhoff & Mourot*	...	pot	imp & pr	179–
	COLOGNE ...	...	pot	p blue	16—

PALETTE.

	PARIS ... ... *Schlossmacher*	...	h p	p gold	18—

PICKAXE.

	LEEDS	...	pot	p color	1770

PIPE.

	ARNSTADT ...	...	pot	p color	176–
	,, ...	...	,,	,,	,,
	VINCENNES ...	...	h p	,,	178–

ROSE.

CAUGHLEY	h p	p color	1799		
J. Rose & Co.					

DELFT	pot	p blue	1764		
De Roos (the Rose), *Dirk van der Does*					

,,	,,	...	,,	,,	,,	

SCEPTRE.

BERLIN	...	...	h p	p blue	176–	

,, ...	...	...	,,	,,	,,	

,, ...	...	...	,,	,,	,,	

SHELL OR HELMET.

CHINA	...	...	h p	p blue

CHINA ...	...	...	h p	p blue	
" ...	...	...	"	"	

SHIELD.

ANSPACH	...	...	h p	p blue	1718
NYMPHENBERG ...	...	h p	imp	1758
SAVONA	...	...	maj	p	16—

*Sometimes with initials G.
A. G., (?) Gian Anto. Guido-
bono, G. S. & B. C.*

"	...	...	"	"	"
" *Girolamo Salomone*	...	"	"	"

SAVONA	...	...	maj	p	16—
DELFT ...	...	...	pot	p red	17—
VOLKSTADT	...	...	h p	p color	1762
TURIN ...	...	...	maj	p	15—

And Shield alone with Cross.
Arms of Savoy

VIENNA	...	...	h p	imp or p blue	1774

SHIP.

COBRIDGE	...	...	pot	p blue	18—

SQUARE MARKS.

CHINA ...	...	...	h p	p blue	

For other Square Marks, see
Oriental, used also by
WORCESTER and DRESDEN

DRESDEN ... ... *Imitation Oriental*			h p	p blue	17—
,, ...			,,	,,	,,
,, *On Böttger ware* ...			ſ ,,	,,	,,
URBINO ... ... *Orazio Fontana*			maj	p	15—
,, ,, *In Greek Characters*			,,	,,	,,

STAR.

DOCCIA			s p	p color	1735
NOVE			h p	p gold or color	1750
DELFT			pot	p red	

SUN.						
St. Cloud	...	...	pot & s p	p blue	1702
„	...	...	„	„	„
Savona	...	...	maj	„	16—
SWORD.						
Caughley	...	...	h p	p blue	1750
Dresden	...	...	h p	p blue	1726
„	...	...	„	„	1730

DRESDEN		h p	p blue	1770
,, *Marcolini Manager* ...		,,	,,	1796
,, on *White Porcelain—for Sale*		,,	,, scratched through	17—
,, on *imperfect pieces* ...		,,	,,	,,
,, ,, ...		,,	,,	,,
,, ,, ...		,,	,,	،,
,, ,, ...		,,	,,	,,

DRESDEN *Brühl Manager*	...	...	h p	p blue	1750
,,	...	...	,,	,,	17—
ELBOGEN	...	...	h p	imp	1810
MONTREUIL *Tinet*	...	...	,,	p blue	18—
TOURNAY	...	...	s p	p gold or blue	175—
(?) CAUGHLEY *Attributed to Worcester*	...	...	h p	p blue	177—
WORCESTER	...	...	s p	p blue	17—

WORCESTER	...	...	s p	p blue	17—

TABLE.

CHINA ...	...	...	h p	,,	
,,	...	...	,,	,,	
,, *imitated by* DERBY	...	,,	,,		

TOWER.

TOURNAY	...	...	s p	p blue	175

	Vincennes	..	...	s p	p color	1/—

TRIANGLE.

	Bow, Chelsea & Derby	...		s p & h p	p gold & color & imp & inc	17—
	Bristol	...	...	h p & bis	imp	18—
	Doccia	...	...	s p	p gold & imp	1735
	Korzec	...	...	h p	p blue	1803
	Nymphenberg	...	...	h p	p blue	1758
	Quimper Hubaudière	...	...	pot	imp	1809

TRIDENT.

Bow				s p	p blue	173—
„				„	„	„
„ the triangle imp ...				„	„	„
CAUGHLEY				h p	p blue	17—
CAFFAGIOLO				maj	„	15—
Also attributed to Faenza & Gubbio						
SWANSEA				h p	imp	18—
And one trident						

VASES.

BRISTOL				h p	pr blue	18—
The Cross imp						
JAPAN				h p	imp color	18—

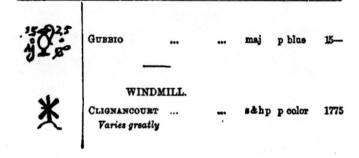

GUBBIO	...	...	maj	p blue	15—

WINDMILL.

CLIGNANCOURT	...	...	s&hp	p color	1775
Varies greatly					

MAJOLICA.

THE manufacture of Italian Pottery—generally known as Majolica or Raffaelle ware—was for many years under the patronage of the Urbino family, and was principally carried on at Urbino, Gubbio, Pesaro, Castel Durante, Faenza and Diruta.

The ware is coarse and bad, but it is valued for the decorations, which are from designs by Raffaelle, Michael Angelo, Guilio Romano, and other great masters; and some are thought to be painted with their own hands.

Marryat says: "It was the usual custom for the Artists to write the title of the subject, in blue characters on the back of the dish, but rarely to affix their names and place of abode." The examples given will, it is hoped, be sufficient for the identification of such marks as may be met with in duplicate, those that are given in type are too large for engraving in a small handbook.

MAJOLICA.

BASSANO, Venetia 1540
Also with the signature of *Antonio Terchi* and
B°· Terchj

CAFFAGIOLO, Tuscany 1507
The ordinary mark is thus made, it is S. P. in s
monogram, sometimes the P is alone given.

,, The trident is used both with and without
above. The name is also signed *In Gafagolo*   ,,

,, This mark is also attributed to *Faenza* and
Gubbio ... ... ,,

,, (?) for *Gafagiolo* ... ... ,,

,, ... ,,

,, ... ,,

1524 ʒn Caſtel Du ꞓunte	CASTEL DURANTE, Urbino ... ... founded 1361		
	The earliest known date is ... 12 Sep., 1508		
	Sebastiano d' Marforio signs and dates a piece in 1519		
	Francesco Durantino „ „ 1533		
Fatto in Botega *di Piccolpasso*	„ The Chevalier *Piccolpasso* was director of a factory about 1550		
In Castello *Duranto*, 1841.	„ On Modern Ware, in imitation of the old		
👑	CASTELLI, Naples ... ... 14—		
	So attributed by Passeri ... ... 16—		
𝒮𝒿𝓈ᵗ	„ *Saverio Grue.* Also initials and name ... 17—		
L. G. P.	„ *Luigi Grue* ... ••• ••• ••• „		
	„ *Fraᵒ· Antᵒ· Grue* ••• ••• ... 1722		
G. Rocca di *Castelli*, 1732.	„ ... ••• ••• ... 1732		
Gentili P.	„ ••• ••• ••• ... 17—		
·1545· *in deruta* ꞓrate fecit	DIRUTA, Papal States ... ... 15—		
	Other varieties of this signature are found		

jnderuta 1554	DIRUTA, Papal States	15—
C	"	16—
IC	"	"
$	" Given by Darcel as a mark of this factory ...	"
	FAENZA	
	On one of the earliest pieces of Majolica known	1475
DON GIORGIO 1489	" (?) Gubbio. Supposed to be *Maestro Giorgio*	14—
E f	" Many varieties of the letter F are found ...	"
Fata in Faenza In Caxa Pirota	" *Casa Piroto*—The name of a factory of Faenza	15—

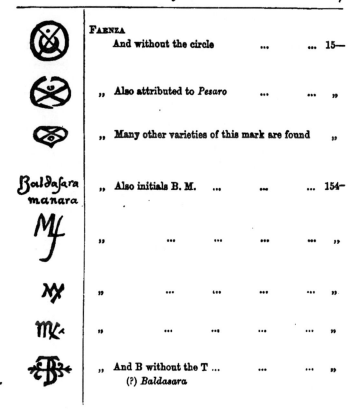

FAENZA And without the circle		...		...	15—
,, Also attributed to *Pesaro*		...		...	,,
,, Many other varieties of this mark are found					,,
,, Also initials B. M.	...		...	...	154—
,,	...	...	...	...	,,
,,	...	...	...	...	,,
,,	...	...	...	...	,,
,, And B without the T ... (?) *Baldasara*		...		...	,,

ⓑ	FAENZA				
	Attributed to *Baldasara*	•••		•••	15—
(mark)	,,	•••	•••	•••	•••	,,
F. R.	,, In a square, and initials only	•••		•••	,,
	FLORENCE, Tuscany	...	...	...	14—
	Luca della Robbia and his family made their				
	famous ware here until about	...		...	1560
BL. 1429 FAC-EBAT	This mark and another, LR FA, 1454, is attributed to *Luca*, but both are very doubtful				
F.	,, A late mark on fine pottery	•••		•••	17—
FI	,, ,, (?) for *Firenze*	•••		•••	,,
	FORLI	•••	...	...	15—
Fata in Forli, 1542.	Also without date, and with signature of *Leucadius Solombrinus*, 1555				
I la Botega d M° Jero da Forli.	,,	•••	•••	•••	•••	,,

GENOA ... ... 15—
The beacon is well known, it varies very much

„ Given by Demmin ... ... 16—

GUBBIO, Urbino ... ... 14—
Giorgio Andreoli, afterwards known as *Maestro Giorgio,* first used the beautiful metallic lustre which caused the Gubbio ware to be so valued

G
A   „ Also ascribed to him ... ... „

„ „ 1519

„ „ ... ... „

„ „ 1525

GUBBIO—*Maestro Giorgio*						
	B A, Merchants' mark...		...		...	1528
	"	...	...	...	...	1532
	" With merchants' mark		...		...	15—
	"	...	...	...	...	"
	"	...	...	...	...	"
	" Attributed to *Maestro Gillio*		...		...	"
	" *Vincentio* or *Cencio*, son of Mº· Giorgio			...		"

GUBBIO				
Also N. G. ...	...	...	...	15—
„ (?) *Maestro Perestino.* Also signature in full			„
„ (?) *Salimbene*	...	...	...	16—
„ (?) *Hipollito Rombariotti*	...	...	„
„ (?) *Rovigo* ...	...	...	...	15—
„	...	...	...	...	„
LODI, Lombardy ...	...	...	...	16—
And with the initials only				

M. A. I. M.

Milano F✛C	MILAN, Lombardy	...	...	... 17—	
P R 𝓕 *Mil=no*	„	...	...	...	„
G. R.	„ On modern pottery	...	...	... 18—	
M. 1627.	MONTELUPO, Tuscany	...	...	... 16—	
	Variously written				
M^o L^o 1639.	„ With signature *Raffaello Girolamo*				
	„ Given by Jacquemart ...		...	p black	
	(?) Wolf's brush			modern	
1524	NAPLES	...	...	...	15—
	„ Crown of various shapes, some-				
	times B. C.	...	...		16—

F.D.V N	NAPLES. ,, *And Ferdinando del Vecchio Napoli* imp in full 17—
H.F	,, So attributed
HF	,, ... 17—
Giustiniani IƱN	,, *Giustiniani Brothers* ... ... imp 17—
G	,, ,, ... ·, ,, & p color
☾	,, And in outline ... ... p blue 17—
Padva.	PADUA, Venetia ... ... 15— With date, 1548
A. Padoa.	,, ,, 1563

In Pesaro.	PESARO ... ... 13—				
	With dates, 1542 to 1765				
Fatto in Pesaro	„ „ ••• ••• ••• ... 15—				
I.P	„ Doubtful				
VFO	„ (?) *Giovanni Vejaso* 1542				
Ravena.	RAVENNA				
	Between two flourishes ... ••• ... 16—				
In Arimin 1535.	RIMINI ... ••• ... ... 15—				
	Stiffly written				
In Rimino 1535.	„ ••• ... ••• ... 1535				
Fato in Ariminensis 1635.	„ ••• ••• ••• ... 1635				
Fatto in Roma da Gio Pavlo Savino M.D.C.	ROME ... ... ••• ••• ... 16—				
	Pencilled in oval ... ••• ... 1600				
In Roma.	„ Pencilled and impressed ... ••• „				

Alma Roma 1623.	ROME.	
	,,	16—
	SAVONA, Genoa ... ... 16—	
	(?) *Guidobono* ... ... ,,	
	,, *Girolamo Salomone* ... ... 16—	
	,, ,, ... ,,	
	,, ... ,,	
	,, With initials G. A. G. (*Gian Ant°. Guidobono*) and G. S. (*Salomone*) & B. C. ... ... ,,	

	SAVONA, Genoa ...	...	...	...	16—
	,,	...	...	...	16—
Fata i Siena.	SIENA, Tuscany ...	...	...	...	15—
	With signatures of *M° Benedetto*				
Bar Terese Roma.	,, *Bartolomeo Terensio Romano*	...		...	1727
F. C.	,, Also in monogram *Ferdinando Maria Campani* ...	...	...	...	1733
	TREVISO, Lomardy	...	...	...	15—
Treviso.	In circle ...	...	...	...	,,
N.	,, So attributed	...	...	...	,,
	TURIN, Piedmont	...	...	...	15—
	And Shield alone with Cross. Arms of Savoy				

Fatta in Torino	TURIN, Piedmont	...	...		...	1577
Fabrica Reale di Torino 1737.	,,	...	...	...	...	17—
GRATAPAGLIA FE:TAVR	,, So attributed	...	...	...	,,
·1531·	URBINO	...	...	...	...	14—
·f·X·A·R· ·T Urbino.	*Francesco Xanto Avelli da Rovigo*	...	p colour	15—
1532- *fXato*·A·R· *Turbino·*	,,	,,	...	,,	,,
F:o X: *Rou:*	,,	,, .	...	,,	,,
·1539 X:	,,	,,	...	,,	,,
X·N	,, X in blue, N in red lustre, probably *Vicentio's* mark					

E

URBINO	...	...	...	...	15—
Francesco Xanto Avelli					
,, *Orazio Fontana*	...	...	...		15—
,, ,, *Urbino Fecit*	...	...			
,, ,, In Greek characters	...	,,			
, ,, ...	...	...	,,		
,, A similar mark dated 1549	...	...	,,		
,, *Nicolo d' Urbino.* About 1530					
also signed *Nicolo di V.*					

	URBINO	
	Nicolo d' Urbino	15—
	Geronimo Vrbino, with date	1583
T. R. F. 1587.	,, ...	1587
	,, Also with initials E F B, dated	1594
F. G. C.	,,	
Alf. P. F. Vrbini, 1606.	,, Alfonso Patanazzi. Also name in full ...	1606
A.P.	,, ,, ...	,,
F.P. 1617	,, Francesco Patanazzi. Also name in full ...	1608
	,, Vicenzio Patanazzi, aged 12 years ...	1619
	,, (?) Luca Cambiasi, of Genoa	16—
B. F. V. F.	,, (?) Battista Franco Urbini Fecit	,,
VR	,, ...	,,

FACTORIES.

A.N.	ALTENROLHAU near Carlsbad, Germany ... ... *A. Nowotny, Director*	pot & h p	imp	1829
Amstel.	AMSTEL,Oude,near Aı sterdam, Holland	h p	p blue	1782
Amstel	AMSTEL, Niewer	h p	p blue	18—
	AMSTERDAM, Holland ...	h p	p blue	1772
	„ „ ... „	„	„	„
	„ *A. Daeuber, Director* ...	„	„	178—

	AMSTERDAM, Holland *Hartog & Brandeis*	...	pot	p color	1780
	ANDENNES, France *B. Lammens & Co.*	...	pot	imp	18—
	„ „ *A. Der Vander Wœrt*	...	„	„	„
	ANSPACH, Bavaria *And other varieties of the A, sometimes like crossed swords*	...	h p	p blue	1718
	„ *The Eagles and Shields vary very much, and sometimes are used without the letter*	„	„	„	„
	„ „	„	„	„	„

Anspach	...	...	h p	p blue	1718
„ And Frankenthal J. A. Hannong	...		„	„	„
Aprey, France	...	...	pot	p black	1750
„ „	...	...	„	„	„
Arnstadt, Germany		...	pot	p color	176–
„ „		...	„	„	„
Arras, France	...	...	s p	p blue	1782
Baden-Baden, Germany Widow Sperl	...		h p	p gold or color	1753

BADEN-BADEN, Germany	...	h p	p gold or color	1753
Widow Sperl				
,,	,,	...	,,	,,	,,
BAYREUTH, Bavaria	...	pot	p black	15—
,,	,,	...	pot	p blue	15—
,,	,,	...	h p	p	1744

BERLIN, PRUSSIA.

Established by W. G. Wegeley, in 1751, and purchased by Frederick the Great, in 1763. Pott, a chemist at this factory, claims the invention of transfer printing on porcelain.

BERLIN, Prussia.

,, *Wegeley*	...	...	h p	p blue	1751

BERLIN, Prussia					
„ *Royal Factory.* *Many forms of sceptre*	...	h p	p blue	176–
„	„	•••	„	„	„
„	„	•••	••	„	„
„ *Königliche Porzellen Manufactur*	•••	„	„	1830
„ „	•••	„	p r	1850
	This Eagle is also used by Schuman, of Moabit, with names				
„ *Frequently painted in green or gold over the sceptre mark, on damaged pieces*	...	„	„	18—

℞	BORDEAUX, France *Lahens & Rateau*	...	h p	p color	18—
BlaR	BOURG-LA-REINE, France	...	s p & pot	p blue	1773
oP	„	„	...	h p	„	„
	„ *Le Chappelet*	„	...	„	p	„

BOW.

This factory was established about 1735, but did not become celebrated until many years later.

	Bow	...	...	s p	p blue	173
	„	...	...	„		„

Bow	... ...	s p	p blue	173-
„	*The form and position of the sword vary*	„	p red & gold	„
„	*The triangle has long been considered a Bow mark, but recent researches have rendered it doubt-ful, it is often hard to say if it is a Bow or Triangle, the latter is now proved to have been used at* CHELSEA *and* DERBY		imp inc p gold & color	„
„	*Triangle, imp* ...	„	p blue	„
„	... ...	„	„	„
„	*A. B. F. G. & K. are also found, probably work-men's marks*	„	„	„
„	*Also* BRISTOL ...			

ELERS	BRADWELL	...	...	pot	imp	1696
✛ ✗	BRISTOL					
	Founded by Richard Champion			h p	p color	1773
王	,, *And other imitations of Oriental marks*		...	,,	,,	,,
✛ B	,,	•••	•••	,,	,,	,,
B₇	,,	•••	•••	,,		,,
	,, *The cross impressed*		...	h p	pr blue	18—
	,,	•••	•••	,, & biscuit	imp	,,
Tᵒ	,, *For Tebo, the modeller. Many other workmen's marks are found*		...	,,	inc	17—

Crettes de Bruxelle rue D'Arenberg 191	BRUSSELS, Belgium L. Cretté	...	h p	p color	1791
LC.	„ „	...	...	„	P „	„
🌷 *B*	„	...	...	„	P „	18—
THOMAS TOFT	BURSLEM, Staffordshire And Ralph Toft	...	pot	in relief	1670
William Sans.	„	...	...	„	imp	167–
R. Shawe.	„	...	...	„	„	173–
N EDGWOOD. *Wedgwood.*	„	...	...	„	„	175–
Aaron Wood.	„	...	...	„	„	„
Enoch Wood.	„	...	...	„	„	· 1783
Wood & Caldwell.	„	...	...	„	„	1790
Steel.	„	...	...	„	„	18—

BUEN RETIRO (Madrid), Spain *Attributed to Royal Factory, Charles III., but probably* LUDWIGSBURG	s p & pot	p color	176–
,, *The Capo di Monte mark is found on early pieces*	,,	,,	,,
,, *And M only*	,,	,,	,,
CAEN, France	h p	p red	1793
Also in capitals			
CALDAS, Portugal ...	pot	imp	18—
Mafra, maker. Imitations of Palissy ware			
CAPO DI MONTI, Naples ...	s p	p blue	1736
And various other forms of Fleur de lys			
,, *Ferdinand IV, patron* ...	,,	p red or blue & imp.	1759

Capo di Monti, Naples				
„ This factory has success-fully imitated old ma-jolica	s p	p color	1759
„ Ferdinandus Rex ...	„	p color	1780
Casemène, France ... ... Lafléchere and Paillaird	pot	imp	18—
Castleford, near Leeds ... D. Dunderdale	pot	imp	1790
Caughley, Shropshire ... Established in 1750, by Brown, taken in 1772 by Thomas Turner.	h p	p blue	1750
„ Crescent marked thus is often mistaken for D and attributed to Duesbury of Derby.		p blue	
„	„	„	„

D. D. & Co.
CASTLEFORD
POTTERY.

SALOPIAN.

S

CAUGHLEY, Shropshire	...	...	h p	p blue	1750
TURNER.	„	...	...	h p & pot	imp	1772
„	...	...	h p	p blue	17—
„	...	...	„	„	„
„ *And other numerals thus treated, to resemble oriental marks*	...	„	p blue	177-
„ *(?) Turner, attributed to* WORCESTER	...	„	„	„
„ *Ross & Co.* ...	...	„	p color	1799
CHANTILLY, France *Also with name*	...	s p	p blue and imp	1725

CHELSEA.

This factory, established in the 17th century, acquired little celebrity until about 1750, when the modelling and beauty of the paste rendered its productions equal to those of any foreign factory.

CHELSEA	...	...	a p	imp	174–
,,	... *The best quality in gold*	...	,,	p gold or red	174–
,,	...	...	,,	,,	,,
,,	...	...	,,	,,	,,
,,	...	...	,,	,,	,,
,,	...	...	,,	,,	,,

CHELSEA	s p	p gold or red & imp	1745
And with name in full			
CLIGNANCOURT, near Paris ...	h & s p	p color	1775
This varies very much			
„ Monogram of the Patron, Louis Stanislas Xavier, Comte de Provence	h p	st red	„
„ Porcelaine de Monsieur	„	„	1780
COALPORT, or COALBROOK DALE, Shropshire	h p	p blue	1787
„ And C. Dale	„	„	„
„	„	„	„
„	„	„	18—

	COALPORT, or COALBROOK DALE, Shropshire					
	,,	...	...	h p	p blue	18—
	,, Caughley, Swansea, Nant- garw, united 1821				,,	1861
Voyes.	COBRIDGE, Staffordshire	...	pot	imp		1773
	,, ,,	...	,,	p blue		18—
	COLOGNE, Germany	...	pot	p blue		1589
	,, ...	...	,,	,,		16—
	,, ...	...	,,			,,

	COLOGNE, Germany	...	pot	p blue	16—
	„ *Cremer* ...	...	„	„	17—

Given by M. Demmin.

„　B. M.	L. W., 1573.
„　B. V., 1574.	M. G., 1586.
„　F. T., 1559.	M. O.
„　F. V. O., 1543.	S. M.
„　I. E., 1539.	W. R.
„　I. R., 1588.	W. T.
„　Kᵒ· R., 1598.	

	COPENHAGEN, Denmark ...		h p	„	1772
	The Sound and great and little Belts				
	„	... ...	„	p color	„

CRIEL.	CRIEL, France	pot	imp	178–
	Also with monogram of Stone-Coquerel and Le Gros of Paris			
.D	DAMM, Germany	h p	p blue	17—

DELFT, HOLLAND

Potteries were established here at a very early date; it is said that fine ware was produced in 1480, nothing certain is known before 1614, when a patent was granted to Claes Janssén Wytman's, for making porcelain, probably fine pottery.

DELFT, Holland				
„ The ALPHA *De Grieken A.*	*Mark registered*			1764
J. T. Dextra or Dikstraat	pot	p blue		„
„ ... ... „	„	„

DEX	DELFT, Holland	pot	p blue	1764
Z:DEX	,, *Zoon Dextra*	,,	,,	1765
	,, *On ware with same pat-* *terns as that with first* *mark*	,,	,,	
	,, *The works were carried on* *by Jacobus Halder* *Adriens Zoon in 1765...*	,,	,,	,,
I. H. D.	,, (?) *Jacobus Halder* ...	,,	p blue	
	,, *Cornelis van Os had the* *works in 1767*			
	,, The AXE. *De Byl* ...			reg 1764
	,, *Justus Brouwer* ...	,,	p blue	,,
	,, ,, ...	,,	,,	,,
	,, ,, ...	,,	,,	,,

˙* İB	DELFT, Holland ... ... *Justus Brouwer.* *This is also attributed to* *A. Kielle, of the White* *Star.*	pot	p blue	1764
	,, The CLAW. *De Klaauw* *Lambertus Sanderus.*	,,	,,	reg 1764
	. ,, *This mark is so varied* *that it is usually " un-* *known." It has been* *called The Griffin!*	,,	,,	,,
	,, ,, ...	,,	,,	,,
	,, ,, ...	,,	,,	,,
O.S.K A	,, The DOUBLE PITCHER. *De Dubbelde Schenkkan* *Thomas Spaandonck...*	,,	,, ,, 1764

	DELFT, Holland					
2 Fortuyn	„ FORTUNE. *T' Fortuyn*... Pieter van der Briel	*T' Fortuyn*...	pot	p blue	reg 1691
x *Fortuijn*	„	„	...	„	„	„
⊕ PB	„	„	...	„	„	„
PB	„	„	...		„	„
PVDB	„	„	...	„	„	„
W.V.DB	„	*Weduwe v. d. Briel*	...	„	„	1764
J. H. F. Int. Fortuyn.	„	...	...	„		
I. D. A.	„	The GOLDEN BOAT. *In der vergulde Boot Johannes der Appel*	*In*	„		„ 1764
De Blompot.	„	The GOLDEN FLOWERPOT. *De vergulde blompot* ... P. Verberg		„		„ 1764

THART	DELFT, Holland				
	„ The HART. *T' Hart* ...	pot	p blue	reg 1764	
HVMD	„ *Hendrik van Middeldijk*	„	„	„	
MP	„ The METAL POT ...			1639	
	De Metaale Pot				
MP	*Lambertus Cleffius* ...	„	„	„	
	Pieter Paree ...	„		„ 1764	
GVS	„ The old MOOR'S HEAD ...	:„		„ „	
	In t' oude Moriaans Hofft				
	„ *Geertruy Verstelle* ...	„	„	„	
E. B. S.	„ The young MOOR'S HEAD	„		„ „	
	T'jongue Moriaans Hofft				
	Widow of Pieter Jan				
	v. d. Hagen				
	„ Probably a mark of one or				
	other of these factories	„	p color		
D AW	„ The PEACOCK. *De Paauw*	„	p blue	„ 1651	
	Jacobus de Milde ...			„ 1764	
D AW	„	„		„	

paüw	DELFT, Holland				
	,, *Jacobus de Milde* ...	pot	p blue	1764	
I.D.M	,, ,, ...	,, .	,,	,,	
CB D ŻRV	,, (?) *Cornelis Boumeester*	,,	,,	17—	
P.V	,, The PORCELAIN BOTTLE			reg 1764	
	De Porceleyne Fles				
	,, *Pieter van Doorne* ...	,,	,,	,,	
VD	,, ,, ...	,,	,,	,,	
Duyn	,, The PORCELAIN PLATTER				
	De Porceleyne Schootel				
	,, *Johannes van Duyn* ...	,,	,,	,,	,,
PVM / 6	,, The ROMAN				
	De Romeyn				
	,, *Petrus van Merum* ...	,,	,,	,,	,,
PM	,, ,, ...	,,	,,	,,	

DELFT, Holland				
„ *Jan van der Kloot Janzoon took the factory*	pot	p blue	1764
„ The ROSE ... ... *De Roos*			reg 1764
„ *Dirk van der Does* ...	„	„	„
„ • „ ...	„	„	„
„ The THREE BELLS *De drie klokken*			
„ *W. van der Does* ...	„	„	„ „
This varies so much that it is "unknown" ...	„	„	„
„	„	„	„
„ Doubtful	„	„	

	DELFT, Holland					
	,, The THREE PORCELAIN BOTTLES *De drie Porceleyne fleschjes*					reg 1764
℔	,, *Hugo Brouwer* ...	pot	p blue			,,
Hooren.	,, The THREE PORCELAIN BARRELS *De drie Porceleyn astonnen*	,,	,,	,,	,,	
*H*V*H*	,, *Hendrick van Hoorn* ...	,,	,,			,,
	,, The TWO SHIPS ... *De twee Sheepjes*			,,	,,	
ℛ	,, *Ant. Pennis*	,,	,,			,,
	,, The TWO WILD MEN ... *De twee wildemans*			,,	,,	
WVB	,, *Widow of Willem van Beek*	,,	,,			,,
LPK	,, The WATER CAN ... *De Lampetkan*			,,	,,	
	,, *Widow of Gerardus Brouwer*	,,	,,			,,
L P Kan	,, ,, ...	,,	,,			,,

	DELFT, Holland						
✳ A·K·	,,	The WHITE STAR	...				reg 1764
		De witte ster					
	,,	*A Kielle*	...	...	pot	p blue	
²A̲K̲	,,	,,	•••	•••		,,	,,
A.K.	,,	,,	...	...	,	,,	
A̲K̲ A̲K̲	,,	,,	...	. •••		,,	,,
	,,	,,	•·•	•••		,,	,,
⊼K	,,	,,	•••	•••		,,	,,
A̲K̲	,,	,,	*And other variations*			,,	,
A̲B̲ ANNO 1794	,,	(?) *Van der Bosch*	•••	—		,,	1774
B t	,,	*Berghem*	•••	•••		,,	

	DELFT, Holland				
$\overset{\bullet}{B}$	,, Isaak Brouwer	...		p blue	1750
BVDD	,, (?) Van der Does	...		,,	
L b	,, (?) Van Dammelar	...		,,	
SE	,, Suter van der Even	...		,,	1580
VE	,, ,,	...		,,	,,
VE	,, ,,	...		,,	,,
VE	,, ,, so attributed				,,
(KEY YY 3)	,, Martinus Gouda	...		reg 1675	
H A	,, Antoni Ter Humpelin	...		p color	1650

	DELFT, Holland				
	,, Q. *Kleynoven*	...		p blue	reg 1680
	,, *Jan Kuylich the younger*			,,	,,
	,, ,,	...		,,	,,
	,, ,,	...		,,	,,
	,, ,,	...		,,	,,
	,, *Johannes Mesch*	...		,,	,,
	,, *Cornelis Keyser* *Jacobus Pynaker and* *Adrien Pynaker*	...		,,	,, ,,
	,, ,,	...		,,	,,
	,, ,,	...		,,	,,

	DELFT, Holland				
	,, Keyser & Pynaker	...		p blue	1680
	,, (?) Pynaker ...	...		,,	,,
	,, ,, ...	...		,,	
	,, Jan Steen ...	...		,,	1650
	,, Samuel Piet Roerder	...		p color	,,
	" Willem van der Velde	...		,,	1660
	,, Abraham Verboom	...		,,	1680
	,, Piet Viseer ...	...		,,	1769
	,, (?) Philip Wouvermans	...		,,	16—

ΛVH DɈM ZD *1773*	DELFT, Holland
	UNKNOWN MARKS	...		p color	1773
B:P	,,	,,	...	p blue	
ℤ/180	,,	,,	...	,,	
G·B·C	,,	,,	...	p red	
GↃG *1779*	,,	,,	...	,,	1779
ℋ·S·Ↄ ℛ	,,	,,	...	,,	
Ↄℛℱ 1182	,,	,, (?)	*In T' Fortune*	p blue	

	DELFT, Holland					
ɪW	UNKNOWN MARKS			...	p blue	
J.J.8	,,	,,	...	...	,,	
K	,,	,, (?) *Jan Kuylich*			,,	
KVK 1731	,,	,,	...	...	p blue	1731
MVC 4	,,	,,	...	...	p color	
P 15	,,	,,	...	...	p blue	
R	,,	,,	...	...	p brown	
RJ	,,	,,	...	...	p blue	
18	,,	,,	...	...	,,	
	,,	On ware painted in the style of Majolica. An imitation of a Savona mark.			p red	17—

米囙⼈	Delft, Holland	p red	
二 訇 伝 奋 韮 占	„ *Imitation of the "Six mark." On ware painted with Oriental patterns*	p blue	18—

From M. Demmin.

A. D. W. A°· 1769.	D. M.	I. G. V. 1768.	R. or A. R.
A. I., 1663.	D. V. X. I., 1540.	I. H. F. 1480.	R. T. C.
B. P.	G. D., 1605.		S. B. + + 1742.
B. V. S., 1702.	G. V. M.	I. V. L., 1662.	
D., 1540.	H. N. I.	J. G.	S. L., 1650.
D. · ―― 12	I. G.	J. V. L.	S. M., 1725.
B.	22½	M. Q.	V. H., 1620.

DECORATORS.

Aalines.
C. Boumester, 1680.
J. Dam.
S. Dam.
J. Decker, 1698.
Heindering Waanders, 1781.

J. Kuwyt.
J. Meer.
Meer. } *Jan v. d. Meer de Delft*
A. Veerhart de Gouda.
C. Zachtleven Fa. 1650.

DERBY.

Founded in 1751, by W. Duesbury, who, in 1770, pur-chased the Chelsea Works, and, in 1784, removed the moulds and models to Derby; also Bow, 1776.

DERBY ... ... Duesbury.	s p	p red	1756
DERBY CHELSEA	s p	p gold or red	1770
,, *Later in lilac, then in red*	,,	p gold	177–
CROWN DERBY ... ... *Also without the dots— with monogram D K*	h p	p red or violet	1780
Duesbury and Kean ...	,,	,,	1798
,, *Also with* 𝔅 *in old English type*	,,	,,	1780

DERBY				
,, *In imitation of the Sèvres mark*	h p	p red or violet	1798
,, *In imitation of the Chinese*	,,	p blue	,,
,, *Probably a workman's mark*	,,	,, & imp	,,
,, *And in oval*	h p	pr color }	1815 1839
,, *Stevenson & Hancock* ...	h p	p color	186–
Joshua Heath. ,, *Cockpit Hall* ...	pot	imp	1760
DOCCIA, near Florence, Italy *Various star marks*	s p	p color	1735
,, ...	,,	imp & p gold	,,

GINORI.	Doccia, near Florence, Italy...	s p	imp	1735
	The founder's name			
	The Capo di Monti moulds			
	were transferred here			
	about			1821

DRESDEN, Saxony.

The first European Porcelain manufactory, established by Augustus II. in 1709, under the management of Böttger.

	DRESDEN, Saxony			
	,, *Augustus Rex, founder* ...	h p	p blue	1709
	,, *The Caduceus (sale mark)*	,,	,,	1712 to 1720
	,, *Böttger ware* ...	,,		about 1718
	,, ,, ...	,,	,,	,,
	,, *And other square marks in imitation of oriental*	,,	,,	,,

	DRESDEN, Saxony...	...	h p	r blue	1720	
	Herold, *manager*					
	,, ,,	...	,,	,,	1726	
	,, ,,	...	,,	,,	1730	
	,, ,,	...	,,	,,	1739	
	,, Brühl, *manager*	...	,,	,,	1750	
	,, ...	...	,,	,,	17—	
	,, Meissen *porzellen manu-*		,,	,,	,,	
	factur. Also without					
	the swords.					

	DRESDEN, Saxony... ...	h p	p blue	17—
	Early mark			
	,, *Sachsische porzellen manu-*	,,	,,	1750
	factur			
	,, *Königliche porzellen manu-*	,,	,,	17—
	factur			
	,, ...	,,	,,	1770
	,, *Marcolini, manager* ...	,,	,,	1796
	,, *On white porcelain (per-*	,,	p blue	17—
	fect), for sale.		scratched	
			through	
	,, *On imperfect pieces* ...	,,	,,	,,

	DRESDEN, Saxony...	...	h p	p blue	17—
	On imperfect pieces			scratched	
				through	
	,, *On faulty table goods*	...	,,	,,	,,
	,, ,,	...	,,	,,	,,
	,, ,,	...	,,	,,	,,
	A modern imitation of	,,	p blue	18—	
	early mark		& imp		
	ELBOGEN, Bohemia	...	h p	imp	1810
	ETRURIA—see *Wedgwood*				
Wedgwood&Co	FERRYBRIDGE, near Buralem	,,	,,	1796	
			& pot		

FLORENCE, Italy ...		s p	p color	1580
This varies very much				
,, *The arms of the Medici family. Rare mark.*		,,	,,	15—
FRANKENTHAL, Bavaria ...		h p	p blue	1754
The arms of. Hannong of Strasbourg, removed here, 1753.				
,, *Paul Hannong* ... *Also J. A. H., in monogram*		,, & pot	,, & inc	,,
,, *Carl Theodore, patron* ...		h p	p blue	1761
FULDA, Germany ... ... *Fürstlick Fuldaisch*		h p	p blue	1763 to 1780

FULDA, Germany	h p	p blue	1763
On figures.			
FURSTENBERG, Germany ...	h p	p blue	1750
„ *The F varies very much*...	„	„	„
GERA	h p	p blue	1780
GOTHA	h p	p blue	175–
„ *Rothenberg, the founder*	„	„	„
GROSBREITENBACH ...	h p	p color	1770
„ *Sometimes a mere flourish*	„	„	„

	HAGUE (THE), Holland	...		h p	p blue	177–
	A *Stork—the Arms of the Town*					
	,,	,,	...	,,	,,	,,
	HALDENSTEBEN, ALT, Germany			h p	imp	17—
	HANLEY					
E. *Mayer.*	,,	...	...	pot	imp	177–
Lakin & Poole.	,,	...	...	,,	,,	,,
Shorthose.	,,	...	...	,,	,,	,,
	,,	,,	...	,,	,,	1776
NEALE & CO.	,,	...	...	,,	,,	1778
J. MEIGH & SONS.	,, *Also Meigh* ...		...	,,	,,	178–
NEELD.	,, *In imitation of Wedgwood*		,,		,,	178–

J. Keeling.	HANLEY ... , ...		pot	imp	179–
Eastwood.	,, W. Baddeley ...		,,	,,	,,
Shorthose & Heath.	,, ...		,,	,,	18—
T. SNEYD, HANLEY.	,, ...		,,	,,	,,
Mason's Ironstone China.	,, Lane Delph, near ...		,,	pr color	1813
	HERCULANEUM—*see* LIVERPOOL.				
HEREND.	HEREND, Hungary ...		h p	p blue	1800
	Also Shield & Crown of Austria, & Shield & Crown of Hungary.				
MF	,, Maurice Fischer ...		,,	,,	1839
[horse mark]	HESSE CASSEL, Germany ...		h p	p blue	1763
HD [crown mark]	HESSE DARMSTADT, Germany		h p	p blue	1756
[crown A mark]	HILDERSHEIM, Germany ...		h p	p blue	1760

HÖCHST, near Mayence, Germany	h p		p gold & color	1720
The arms of the Archbishop of Mayence				
,,	...	...	,,	,,	,,
,, *Dahl*	...	...	pot & h p	p color	1794
KIEF, Russia	...	...	pot	p color	178–
KIEL, Denmark	...	...	pot	p gold or color	177–
Buchwald, Director				
Abr. Leihamer fecit				
,, *Also K. T. G*	...	,,	,,	,,
KORZEC, Poland	...	h p	p blue	1803
,, *The mark varies very much, and is sometimes used with the name*				
KREUZEN, Germany	...	pot	p color	1610 to 1690
Caspar Vest				
Hans Christophe Vest				

J. Lockett.	LANE END OF LONGTON, Staffordshire	...	pot	imp	17—
TURNER.	,,	...	,,	,,	1762
B. Plant.	,,	...	,,	,,	177-
T. Harley, Lane End.	,,	...	pot & h p	imp	1809
May' & Newbd	,, Mayer & Newbold	...	,,	imp & pr color	18—
Bailey & Batkin.	,,	...	pot	imp	18—
LEEDS POTTERY.	LEEDS	...	pot	imp	1770
人	,, ,,	...	,,	p color	,,
人	,, Also with name, Hartley, Green & Co.		,,	imp	,,
Lille	LILLE, France ...	...	pot	p color	1711
D2	,, Dorez ... ... D is also found on soft pasts.		,,	,,	174-
﷼	,,	...	,,	,,	17—

LILLE, France ... ... F. Boussemart.			pot	p color	1729
,, Petit ••• •••			,,	,,	1778
,, Patron, The Dauphin ... Leperre Duroo.			h p	sten & p red	1784
LIMBACH, Saxe-meiningen ...			h p	p red	1761
,, ••• •••			,,	p gold	,,
,, (?) ••• •••			,,	p color	,,
,, ••• •••			,,	,,	,,
LIMOGES, France			h p	p red	1773

J.P **L**	LIMOGES, France	...	pot	p color	18 -
	.J. Pouyat				
IAG ●	LISBON	...	,,	imp	18—
SHAW.	LIVERPOOL	...	,,	,,	17—
Richard Chaffers	,, ...	...	,,	p color	1751
SADLER.	,, *Sadler claims the inven-*		,,	pr color	1754
	tion of transfer printing	& h p			
	on pottery, 1756.				
SADLER & GREEN.	,, ...	...	,,	,,	1756
Reid & Co.	,, ...	...	h p	,,	175—
	,, *Pennington—also name*		pot	imp	1760
P ⅌	*in full*		& h p	p gold	
				or color	
Christian.	,, ...	...	pot	imp	1765
	,, *Herculaneum*	...	pot	,,	1796
	,, *Also name on garter round*		,,	pr color	,,
	a crown				
	,, *Case, Mort & Co.*	...	pot	p color	1833
	A liver—arms of the town.				

Davenport.	LONGPORT	...	...	pot	imp	1793
LONGPORT.	,, *J. Davenport*	. ...	,,	pr red	,,
DAVENPORT (anchor)	,, .	...	...	,,	imp	,,
DAVENPORT STONE CHINA (mark)	,,	...	...	,,	pr blue	1805
LIVERPOOL (anchor)	,,	...	...	,,	imp	18—
Phillips.	,,	...	...	,,	,,	1760
	LOOSDRECHT, near Amsterdam, Holland *Manufactur oude Loosdrecht. Moll, director*			h p	p blne	1772
M : o · L	LOWESTOFT ... ... *No mark used by factory*			s&h p	,,	175—
(crown over T mark)	LUDWIGSBURG, Würtemberg *Initial of Duke Charles, sometimes used without the crown*			h p	p blue	1758

LUDWIGSBURG, Würtemberg *This form is also attributed* *to Madrid*	h p	p blue	1758
,, *An antler—from the arms* *of Würtemberg*	,,	• ,, or red	,,
,, *Also W. R.*	,,	p blue	1806 to 1818
LUXEMBOURG, Belgium ... *Boch, Director*	pot & h p	p color	1806
MADRID—*see* BUEN RETIRO.			
MALTA	pot	imp	18—
MARANS, France ... ... *Jean Pierre Roussencq*	pot	p color	1740
MARIEBERG, Sweden ...	pot & s p	p color	1750
,, ,, ...	,,	,,	,,

MARIEBERG, Sweden *Ehrenreich.*	...	pot & s p	p color	1759
,, ,, ...	...	,,	,,	,,
,, ,, ...	...	,,	,,	,,
MARSEILLES, France *Also with C. & S.*	...	pot	p color	1777
,, *Savy* ...	...	,,	pr ,,	,,
,, *Veuve Perrin*	...	,,	p black	1760
,, *Bonnefoy* ...	...	,,	p color	1769
,, *Robert* ...	...	h p & pot	p black	1777

MEISSEN, near Dresden, Saxony *Böttger*	pot	imp	17—
MENECY VILLEROY, France ... *Duke of Villeroy*	s p	p color & inc	1735
MIDDLESBOROUGH, Yorkshire 20, *the pattern mark*	pot	p blue imp	18—
MONTET, France ... ... *Laurjorois, manager*	pot	imp	18—
MONTPELLIER, France ... *Le Vouland*	pot	imp	18—
MONTREUIL, sous bois, France *Tinet*	h p	p blue	18—
Moscow, Russia ... ... *A. Gardner*	h p	p color	17—
,, ...	,,	,,	,,

ПОПОВЫ	Moscow, Russia ... ... A. Popoff.		...	h p	p color	1830
A1	,, ,, ...	...	,,	,,	,,
R	,, ,, ...	...	,,	,,	,,
ФГ ГУЛИНА	,, *F. G. Fabrica Gospodina (The factory of our Lady) Galena*		h p & pot	imp color	18—
OL	MOUSTIERS, France	...	pot	,,	1686
	Olery ...	...	,,	p color	172-
OL ○ ♡	,, ,, ...	...	,,	,,	,,
Fᵈ ʃ	,, *Féraud* ...	...	pot	p color	178-
(MOUSTIERS G mark)	,, *Guichard* ... *Also the G only*	...	,,	sten in dots	,,
NANTGARW.	NANTGARW, Wales	...	h p	imp & color	1813

NAPLES.—*See* CAPO DI MONTI.				
N	NEVERS, France	pot	p color	15—
4	,, ...	,,	,,	,,
B	,, *Jacques Bourdu* ...	,,	,,	1602
MF	,, *Denis Lefebvre* ...	,,	,,	1636
H·B	,, *Henri Borne* ...	,,	,,	1689
S	,, *Jacques Seigne* ...	,,	,,	17—
F·R	,, *François Rodrigue* ...	,,	,,	1730
R	,, *Tite Ristori*	,,	,,	1850

NEWCASTLE.	NEWCASTLE-ON-TYNE ...	pot	imp	18—
	NIEDERVILLER, near Stras- bourg, France *Baron de Beyerlé, the* *founder*	h p & pot	p blue	1760
	,, *General de Custine* ...	,,	,,	1786
	,, *And other varieties of the* *coronet*	,,	,,	,,
	,, *Lanfray, director* ...	,,	sten	1802
	,, ,, ...	,,	imp	,,
PBC	NIMES, France ... ... *Plantier Boncourant & Co.*	pot	,,	183–
Nove *	NOVE, Italy	h p	p gold or color	1750
NOVE *	,, ...	,,	,,	,,

✶	NOVE, Italy	h p	p gold or color	1750
ᛒᛀ **1550**	NUREMBURG, Germany ...	pot	imp	1550
Hans Kraut '578	„ *Hans Kraut*	„	p blue	1578
ℋℛ	„ „	„	„	„
ℒℒ	„ *George Liebolt* ...	„	„	1667
⬤	NYMPHENBERG, Bavaria ... *The arms of Bavaria*	b p	imp	1758
✡	„	„	p blue	„
⬬	NYON, Switzerland ...	„	„	1790
ℂℳ	„ *Pierre Mülhausen, painter*	„	„	18—

OPORTO, Portugal *Vista Allegre*	...	h p	p gold or color	1790
„ *Manr. Porto. Rocha Soares*		pot	„	„
ORLEANS, France ... *Gerault Daraubert.*	...	h & s p	p color	1753
„ „ ...	...	pot	p color	„
PARIS, France ... *Reverend*	...	pot	p blue	16—
„ *Hannong. Charles Philippe,* *Comte d' Artois, patron.*		h p	p blue	1769
„ *Morel* ...	...	„	„	1773
„ *De la Courtille* ... *Pouyat & Russinger.*		„	„	„
„ „	...	„	„	„

PARIS, France ... ... Gros Caillou.		h p	p color	1773
„	„ *Advenir Lamarre*	„	„	„
„	*P. A. Hannong* ...	„	„	1773
„	*Porcelaine de la Reine* ...	„	p red	1778
„	*Lebœuf. Marie Antoinette, patroness*	„	„	„
„	*Houssel took the factory* ...			1799
„	*Dihl & Guerhard* ... *Duc d'Angouleme, patron*	„	p red	1780
„	„	„	„	„
„	*Also the names in full— together and separate.*	„	„	„
„	*Nast*	h p	at red	1783

Manu^{frs.} de MM^{rs.} Guerhard et Dihl à Paris.

Nast

Dagoty.	PARIS, France	*Dagoty*	...	h p	p red	179–
Feuillet	,,	*Feuillet*	...	...	,,	,,	,,
*j.*P	,,	*J. Petit*	...	...	h p	p blue	1790
C.H	,,	*Chanou*	...	...	,,	p red	1784
	,,	,,	...	...	,,	,,	,,
	,,	*Schlossmacher*	...	,,	p gold	187–
F & R	PERKENHAMMER, near Carlsbad, Austria *Fischer & Reichembach*			h p	p color	1802
P *P*	PINXTON *So attributed, but the factory had no acknowledged marks.*	...	...	sp	,,	1794
♃	PLYMOUTH ,, *The sign of Jupiter*	...	...	h p	p blue	176–

W	PLYMOUTH ... ... *Probably Jupiter carelessly pencilled*	h p	p blue	176-
M. *M:Cookworthy's* *Factory Plymouth* *1770.*	„	h p	p blue	1770
←—o	„ *Doubtful*	„	„	17—
⚓	POPPLESDORF, Germany ...	pot	imp	176-
△	QUIMPER, France ... *Hubaudière.*	pot	imp	1809
Q—r	RAUENSTEIN, Germany ...	h p	p blue	1760
R—g	REGENSBERG or RATISBON ... Germany	h p	p blue	17—
R	„ „	„	„	„

REGENSBERG, or RATISBON, Germany	h p	p blue	17—
ROCKINGHAM—*see* SWINTON			
ROUEN, France	pot	p color	1542
,, ,,	,,	,,	,,
,, *A great many initials are given by Jacquemart, as Rouen marks*	,,	,,	,,
,, ,,	,,	,,	,,
,, ,,	,,	,,	,,
RUDOLSTADT, Germany ... *Hay fork, part of the Arms of Schwartzberg*	h p	p coior	1758

RUDOLSTADT, Germany ...	h p	p color	1758

SAINTES, FRANCE.

Bernard Palissy settled here about 1538 and after unceasing efforts succeeded in producing the well-known pottery called by his name

SAINTES, France	pot	inc	
So attributed			
ST. AMAND, France ...	pot	p	1750
Fauquez, director.			
ST. CLOUD, France ...	s p	imp	1702
„ *J. B. Chicanneau* ...	pot	p blue	1700
„ *When patronised by the king*	„ & s p	„	1702 to 1715

☀	Sᴛ. Cʟᴏᴜᴅ, France ...	pot & s p	p	1715
S:C. T	,, *Trou, director*	,,	,,	1730
﹀	Sᴛ. Pᴇᴛᴇʀsʙᴜʀɢ, Russia ...	h p	p blue	1744
≡	,, ,,	,,	,,	,,
C c	,, ,,	,,	,,	176–
Ǝ	,, *Catherine II.*	,,	,,	1762
Ǝ ПК	,, *Made for the Palace by Paul Korniloffe* ...	,,	,,	,,
♛ П	,, *Paul*	,,	p color	1796

Sᴛ. Pᴇᴛᴇʀsʙᴜʀɢ, Russia ... *Alexander I.*	h p	p color	1801
,, *Nicholas I.*	,,	,,	1825
,, *Brothers Korneloffski* ...	,,	pr ,,	1827
,, *Alexander II.* ...	,,	p ,,	1855
Sᴛ. Sᴀᴍsᴏɴ, France ...	pot	imp	183–
Sᴄᴇᴀᴜx Pᴇɴᴛʜɪᴇᴠʀᴇ, France *Also* S P.	s p	inc	1750 to 1760
,, *Duc de Penthievre. Lord High Admiral, patron*	pot	p blue	1751
,, ...	s p	,,	1753
,, ...	,,	,,	1792

BPATЬEBЪ
Корниловыхъ

Sceaux.

G

SCHAFFHAUSEN, Germany ... pot   p color   1560
   Tobias Stimmer.

S

SCHLAKENWALD, Austria ... h p   ,,   1800

SEVRES, FRANCE.

This Factory was removed from Vincennes in 1756, and, under the patronage of Madame de Pompadour, became the most celebrated in Europe. The soft paste vases, etc., are now invaluable, owing to their form, colour, and artistic decoration.

SEVRES, France.

,, Royal period. Sometimes   s p   p blue   1753
   with crown. The letter
   indicates the year. See
   Table.

,, Hard paste first made   ...   1768

,, Republic ... ...   h & s p   color   1792

,,   ,, And name only ...   ,,   ,,   ,,

MN^{te}
Sèvres

,, National Manufactory ...   h p   st red   1803
   Mark 1804. See Table.

MImp^{le}
de Sèvres

,, Imperial Manufactory ...   ,,   ,,   1806

SEVRES, France	h p	p red sten & imp	1810
,, *Louis XVIII.* ... Dated with the year of the century.	,,	p blue	1814
,, *Charles X.*	,,	,,	1824
,, ,, *On plain ware* ...	,,	,,	1829
,, ,, *On decorated ware*	,,	,,	,,
,, *Louis Philippe. From August to December.*	,,	,,	1830
,, 1830, *to November,* 1834	,,	p color	,,

SÈVRES, France ... ... *Louis Philippe*	h p	p blue	1834
,, ,, *With the above*	,,	imp or pr color	1834
,, ...	,,	,,	,,
,, *On white porcelain* ...	,,	pr green	1833
,, *Republic to 1851* ... *On decorated ware.*	,,	p red	,,
,, *Napoleon III., Emperor*	h p	pr color	1852
,, ,, *The manu- facture of soft paste was revived 1854.*	h & s p	,,	1854
,, *The scratch marks the piece as undecorated.*	,,	pr green	1861

Sèvres.—TABLE OF DATES.

A	1753	T	1772		
B	1754	U	1773	T. 9*	1801
C	1755	V	1774	X*	1802
D	1756	X	1775	11*	1803
E	1757	Y	1776	* The year of the	
F	1758	Z	1777	Republic.	
G	1759	AA	1778		
H	1760	BB	1779	—⋔—	1804
I	1761	CC	1780	⋀	1805
J	1762	DD	1781		1806
K	1763	EE	1782		
L	1764	FF	1783	7	1807
M	1765	GG	1784	8	1808
N	1766	HH	1785	9	1809
O	1767	II	1786	10	1810
P	1768	JJ	1787	o.z. (onze)	1811
Q	1769	KK	1788	d.z. (douze)	1812
		LL	1789	t.z. (treize)	1813
		MM	1790	q.z. (quatorze)	1814
	,,	NN	1791	q.n. (quinze)	1815
		OO	1792	s.z. (seize)	1816
		PP	1793	d.s. (dix-sept)	1817
R	1770	QQ	1794	18	1818
S	1771	RR	1795	19 &c.	1819

The two last figures of the year to present date.

The months are given by numerals—q.z. 10=October, 1814; 19, 1 =January, 1819.

SEVRES.—*Initials and Monograms of Decorators, &c.*		
Asselin	Portraits.	
Girard	Arabesques, Chinese Subjects, &c.	
Boullemier ...	Gilding.	
Bonnier	Borders.	
Barré	Flowers.	
Mde. Ducluzeau ...	Subjects and Portraits.	
Poupart	Landscapes.	
Rocher	Figures.	
Bar	Detached Flowers.	
Boulanger ...	,, ,,	
Baudouin ...	Borders, Ornaments.	
Bulidon ...	Detached Flowers.	
Beranger ...	Figures.	
Castel	Landscapes, Hunting Subjects, Birds.	
Develly	Landscapes and Figures.	
Chabry	Portraits, Pastoral Subjects.	
Commelin ...	Flowers, Wreaths.	

	Sèvres.—*Initials and Monograms of Decorators, &c.*		
C.P.	Chapuis, ainé	...	Flowers, Birds, etc.
D	Dusolle ...	...	Detached Flowers.
DC	Derichsweiler	...	Borders, Arabesques.
D.i.	Didier ...	...	,, ,,
DR	Drand ...	...	Chinese Subjects and Gilding.
DT.	Dutanda	...	Bouquets, Wreaths.
C.	Couturier	...	Gilding.
B	Bulot ...	...	Flowers.
EL.	Leroy ...	...	Gilding.
MR	Richard ...	...	Flowers.
R	Rejaux ...	...	Borders, Wreaths.
ER	Richard ...	...	Flowers.
F	Falot ...	...	Birds, Butterflies, Borders.
f.	Levé ...	...	Flowers and Chinese Subjects.
f.	Pfeiffer ...	...	Detached Flowers.

SEVRES.—*Initials and Monograms of Decorators, &c.*

Fontaine	...	Flowers.
Barrat ...	...	Wreaths, Bouquets.
Barbin ...	...	Borders, Arabesques.
Merigol ...	...	Flowers and Wreaths.
Regnier Ferdinand		Figures, etc.
Fumez ...	...	Flowers and Borders.
Gerard ...	...	Pastoral Subjects.
Georget ...	...	Portraits.
Gremont	...	Wreaths and Flowers.
Hunny ...	...	Flowers.
La Roche	...	Flowers, Trophies.
Hericourt	...	Flowers and Wreaths.
Huard ...	...	Borders, etc.
Prevost ...	...	Gilding.
Jubin ...	...	,,

SEVRES.—*Initials and Monograms of Decorators, &c.*

J.A.	André	...	Landscapes.
jc.	Chapuis, jeune	...	Detached Flowers.
JD	Mde. Chanou	...	Flowers and Borders.
E	Julienne	...	Arabesques.
Jh	Henrion ...	...	Wreaths and Flowers.
J.n.	Chavaux fils	...	Flowers and Gilding.
Jt.	Thevenet fils	...	Borders, &c.
J.t	Trager ...	...	Birds and Flowers.
k.k	*Dodin* ...	...	Figure, Subjects, Heads.
L L	Levé, père	...	Flowers, Birds, Borders.
L3 LB.	Le Bel, jeune	...	Flowers and Wreaths.
L.B.	Le Bel ...	...	Landscapes.
L°	Le Bel, ainé	...	Flowers.
LG. LG.	*Le Guay*	...	Gilding.

SÈVRES.—*Initials and Monograms of Decorators, &c.*

L.G.	Le Gay	...	Portraits.
LGᶜᵉ	Langlacé	...	Landscapes.
LL LL }	Lecot	...	Chinese Subjects.
X	Armand	...	Birds and Flowers.
LP	Mdlle. Parpette	...	Detached Flowers.
LR.	La Roche	...	Bouquets, Flowers and Trophies.
M.	Massy	...	Flowers and Trophies.
M.m	Michel	...	Detached Flowers.
M	Moiron fils	...	„ „
M.	Morin	...	Sea Views, Military Subjects, Cupids.
MB mb }	Mde. Bunel	...	Flowers.
N.	Aloncle	...	Birds, Animals, Trophies.
nq.	Niquet	...	Detached Flowers.
P	Parpette	...	Flowers.
P.	Pierre, ainé	...	Flowers and Bouquets.

	SEVRES.—*Initials and Monograms of Decorators, &c.*
P	Pline ... ... Borders, etc.
Pb	
PB }	Boucot ... ... Flowers, Birds and Arabesques.
L.h.	Philippine ... Flowers, etc.
P.j	Pithou fils ... Flowers, Trophies.
Pt.	Pithou, père ... Historical Subjects.
P7	
p.7. }	Pierre, jeune ... Flowers and Wreaths.
R	Regnier ... ... Subjects.
Rp	Richard ... ... Borders, Arabesques, etc.
Rx	Riocreux ... Landscapes.
RB.	Mde. Maqueret ... Flowers.
RL.	Roussel ... ... Detached Flowers.
S	Merault, ainé ... Borders.
Sc.	Mde. Binet ... Flowers and Wreaths.
ND	Mde. Nouailher ... Detached Flowers.

	SEVRES.—*Initials and Monograms of Decorators, &c.*		
Sh.	Schadre ...	...	Birds and Landscapes.
S.S.p.	Sinsson ...	...	Flowers.
S.H.	Swebach	...	Landscapes, etc.
T.	Binet ,..	...	Flowers.
D.	Vandé ...	...	Gilding and Flowers.
Jt	Mde. Gerard	...	Flowers and Borders.
H.	Hilken ...	...	Pastoral Subjects.
W	Vavasseur	...	Arabesques.
X	Grison ...	...	Gilding.
X	Micaud ...	...	Flowers, Vases.
Y.	*Bouillat*	...	Landscapes and Flowers.
Z.	Joyau ...	...	Detached Flowers.
	UNKNOWN.		
F. C	Figure subjects, finely painted.		
C.A	Do.	do.	
JJ			
L F	} On fine ware, with other marks.		
R.F			

SEVRES.—*Marks of Decorators, &c.*

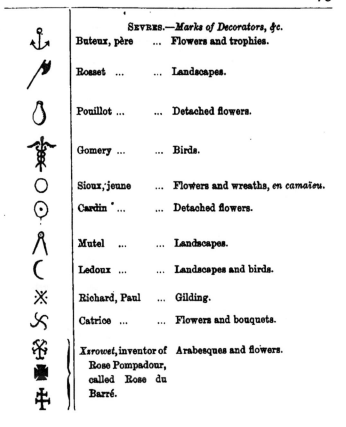

Buteux, père ...	Flowers and trophies.
Rosset	Landscapes.
Pouillot	Detached flowers.
Gomery	Birds.
Sioux, jeune	Flowers and wreaths, *en camaïeu.*
Cardin	Detached flowers.
Mutel	Landscapes.
Ledoux	Landscapes and birds.
Richard, Paul ...	Gilding.
Catrice	Flowers and bouquets.
Xrowet, inventor of Rose Pompadour, called Rose du Barré.	Arabesques and flowers.

	SEVRES.—*Marks of Decorators, &c.*	
Chavaux	...	Gilding.
Tandart ...	...	Flowers and wreaths.
Theodore	...	Gilding.
Fontaine...	...	Trophies, miniatures.
Sioux, ainé	...	Detached flowers.
Raux ...	...	„ „
Choisy ...	...	Flowers and borders.
Taillandier	...	Flowers, etc.
Fontelliau	...	Gilding.
Anteaume	...	Landscapes and cattle.
Viellard ...	...	Figures, trophies and borders.
Thevenet, père	...	Flowers, vases.
Cornaille...	...	Bouquets and flowers.
Chulot ...	...	Trophies and emblems.
(?) Thevenet, père		

5		SEVRES.—*Marks of Decorators, &c.*	
6	Carrier ...	...	Flowers.
9·	Bertrand	...	Detached bouquets.
	Buteux ...	...	Bouquets and wreaths.
9	Merault, jeune	...	,, ,,
2000	Vincent ...	...	Gilding.
⊡	Tardy ...	...	Detached flowers.
✳	Caton ...	...	Pastoral subjects, cupids.
✴	Bienfait ...	...	Gilding.
ϡ	Evans ...	...	Landscapes, birds and insects.
🌳	Bouchet ...	...	Landscapes and figures.
△	Capel le ...	...	Borders, trophies.
△	Buteux fils	...	Pastoral subjects—children.
⚠	Dieu ...	...	Chinese subjects and flowers.
⚱	*Leguay* ...	...	Children—Chinese subjects.
☿	Sinsson ...	...	Flowers and wreaths.

	SEVRES.—*Marks of Decorators, &c.*				
	Noël ... ... Flowers, medallions.				
	Choisy ... ... Flowers, trophies.				
	Aubert ... ... Flowers.				
	Martinet... ... ,,				

The best Painters, &c., are in Italics.

New Hall	SHELTON	pot	pr color	1820
	,, *New Hall Works*			1842
	and name Hackwood.			
M 8.	,, *Miles*	,,	,,	1685
ASTBURY.	,, *Astbury*	,,	imp	17—
R. & J. BADDELEY	,, *Baddeley*	,,	,,	1750
I. & G. RIDGWAY.	,, *Bell Works*	,,	,,	177— to 1816
J. & W. R.	,, ,, ...	,,	,,	to 1854
Sincheny.	SINCENY, France	pot	p color	1733
·S·	,, ...	,,	,,	,,

✦C✦ ✦S✦	SINCENY, France ... *Joseph le Cerf.*	pot	p color	177–
ℳ	,, *Moulin*	,,	,,	1864
SPODE.	STOKE-UPON-TRENT ...	pot h p	imp p red	1770
	,, *Minton*	,,	p color	179–
	,, ,, *On best ware* ...	h p	p gold or color	185–
English Porcelain MINTON	,, ,, ...	,,	pr blue	18—
COPELAND	,, *Copeland. Copeland &* *Garrett, 1833. Cope-* *land, late Spode, 1847.*	,,	pr color	185–
	STRASBOURG, Germany ... *Hannong removed to* *Frankenthal, 1754.*	pot & h p	p blue	17—

.H.	Strasbourg, Germany ...		pot & h p	p blue	17—
м ᴙ	„ *J. Hannong. Paul Hannong.*		„	„	„
Phillips&Co	Sunderland		pot	pr color	1780
	Sunderland Pottery.				
Dixon & Co.	„ „	...	„	„	1805
Moore & Co. Southwark.	„ *Wear Pottery*	...	„	„	180-
CAMBRIAN	Swansea ...	...	h p	p color	178-
SWANSEA	„	... ...	„	imp	18—
SWANSEA	„ *And trident only*	...	„	„	„
Swansea.	„ *And with name, Dyllwyn & Co.*		„	sten red	181-
	Swinton, Rockingham ...		h p	pr red	17—
	The Rockingham Crest. First used about 1824. Brameld, maker.				

BRAMELD.	SWINTON, Rockingham ...	h p & pot	pr red	1807
(mark: 7A)	TOULOUSE, France ... *Fouqué, Arnoux et Cie.*	pot	p color	1820
(mark: kiln symbol)	TOURNAY, France ... *Tour aux oiseaux. Also a potter's kiln.*	s p	p blue	175–
(mark: crossed swords)	,, ...	,,	p gold or blue	,,
(mark)	TOURS, France ... ... *Victor Avisseau.*	h p	p blue	184–
BOOTH.	TUNSTALL ... ... *And name in full—Enoch Booth.*	pot	imp	1750
CHILD.	,, ...	,,	:,	1763
A. & E. Keeling.	,, ...	,,	,,	1770
W. ADAMS.	,, ...	,,	,,	1780

	Turin, Italy	h p	imp	1770
	Vineuf, Dr. Gioanetti.			
	Uzes, France	pot	,,	18—
	François Pichon.			
	Val sous Meudon, France...	,,	,,	179-
	Mittenhof & Mourot.		& pr	
	Varages	pot	p black	1730
			or red	
	Venice, Italy	h p	p red	17—
			or blue	
	,, *Giovanni Marcone* ...	s p	p gold	17—
			or color	
	,, ...	h p	p red	1765
	Vienna, Austria	,,	p blue	1774
	The shape of the shield		or imp	
	varies.			

	VINCENNES, France *The Tower varies.*	...	s p	p color	17—
	„ *Hannong* ...	...	h p	„	178-
	VILLENGEN, Nuremberg *Hans Kraut.*	...	„	„	15—
	VOLKSTADT, Germany	...	h p	„	1762
	VOISONLIEU, France *Jean Ziegler.*	...	pot	st „ & imp	1839
WEDGWOOD.	WEDGWOOD, Burslem and Etruria.		pot & h p	imp	175– 1770
Wedgwood.	„ ...	...	„	„	„
	„ ...	...	„	imp	1768 to 1780

WORCESTER.

This Factory was established, in 1751, by Dr. Wall and others.   The invention of transfer printing on porcelain is attributed to Dr. Wall, but is also claimed for Sadler, of Liverpool, and Dr. Pott, of Berlin..

WORCESTER	...	...	s p	p blue or gold	1751
,,	...	...	,,	,,	,,
,,	Dr. Wall	...	...	,,	,,	,,
,,	Imitation of Chinese marks		,,	p blue or red	,,
,,	Many marks are found in this style, in imitation of Oriental.		s p	p blue or red	17—
,,	...	...	,,	,,	,,

⚔	,,	*Imitation Dresden marks*	s p	,,	17—
⚔	,,	,,	...	,,	,,	,,
⚔	,,	,,	...	,,	,,	,,
C *Flight*	,,	*Flight* ... ... *and name only.*	h p	p blue	1783
👑 *Flight & Barr*	,,	*Flight & Barr* ,, ...	,,	,,	1793
B B	,,	*Barr*	h p	inc	1793
👑 *BFB*	,,	*Barr, Flight & Barr* ... *Also* F B B, *and names in full.*	,,	imp	1807

	Worcester	h p	pr	.18—		
	,, And Chamberlains only.			178–		
	,, Grainger, Lee & Co. ...	,,	,,	1800		
	,, Richard Holdship. A Decorator's mark. He also worked for Derby.	,,	p color	175–		
	Wurzburg, Bavaria ...	,,	p blue	17—		
Absolom Yam.	Yarmouth ... ... A Decorator. Also with name in full.	pot	p	,,		
	Zurich, Switzerland ...	h p	p blue	1759		

W.C.P.

ORIENTAL MARKS.

CHINA.

CHINESE porcelain is said to date from about a century before the Christian era; their pottery is of the greatest antiquity, and, like the porcelain, is of every quality. The oldest example that can now be obtained is of the *Ming* period, though, if the marks could be relied on, there are many pieces of the 10th century still to be found, but marks are so easily imitated, and Chinese potters are so fond of reproducing old patterns with marks complete, that very little reliance can be placed upon them. The best periods of the manufacture of porcelain during the *Ming* dynasty, were—

樂永	Yung-lo	...	1408 to 1424
德宣	Seuen-tih	...	1426 „ 1435
化成	Ching-hwa	...	1465 „ 1487
靖嘉	Kea-tsing	...	1522 „ 1566
歷萬	Wan-leih	...	1573 „ 1619

" Egg Shell " ware was first made in the *Yung-lo* period. The *Seuen-tih* was famous for all sorts of coloured ware.

大明成
年明成
製成

The *Ching-hwa* produced the best ware and the finest decoration. This mark commands larger prices in Europe than any other. The dark rich blue of the *Kea-tching* and the white granulated surface of the *Wan-leih*, are very choice. " Old blue China," or Nankin ware, is from the Imperial factories at King-te-chin—a town of potters named after *King-te*, the Emperor, who first patronized the manufactory in 1004–1007. The ware bore the "six mark" dates until 1667, when they were forbidden by an edict from the governor of the province, lest any piece being broken, the Emperor's name might be profaned by being carelessly thrown on the dust heap. This blue ware was made by direction of the Emperor, who ordered it to be of the colour of the sky after the winter rains.

The marks on Chinese work are seldom either Factory or Painter's marks. M. Stanislas Julien gives the mark of a potter of the *Wan-leih* period, named *Hao-chi-khieou*, who excelled in writing verses and in painting; he appears to have taken religious vows and lived in retire-

道壺
入隱

ment; his mark is *Ou-in-tao-jin*. *Ou*, the hermit. M. Jacquemart mentions a 'six mark,' "sold by *Pei-tching*, made by *Kien-ki*." Some of those given are no doubt makers' names—as *San-yuh*, Mountain of Gems; but the marks most commonly found are in four or six characters, and denote the date of the manufacture.

The 'six mark' may be made out from the table of dates without much trouble, except from badly formed characters, handwriting being as varied in China as elsewhere.

Chinese writing is arranged in columns commencing at the right, reading downwards. If in a horizontal line it reads from right to left.

The first and second characters of the "six mark" show
the dynasty, thus: 大 the third and fourth, the *period*
明
(*nëen haou*), name of the years; the fifth signifies
年 *year*, and the sixth 製 *made:* thus, *Ta-Ming, Hung-
woo, nëen che.* Great Ming (illustrious) dynasty, *Hung-
woo,* years; made. 1368 to 1398. Or arranged thus, *Ta-
Ming, Seuen-tǐh, nëen, che.* Made in the *Seuen-tǐh* period
of the Ming dynasty. 1426 to 1435.

The next example is—

Ta Ts'hing, Yung-ching, nëen, che, Great Ts'hing (pure)
dynasty Yung-ching period. 1723 to 1735. The "four.
mark" is more troublesome, as it does not give the
dynasty it necessitates a search through the whole list of
dates; it is read in the same order, thus: *King-tǐh
nëen, che,* made in the King-tǐh period, about 1004 to
1007.

The square marks called the Imperial Seal, which have
been in use from the beginning of the last century, are
read in the same way; they are written in an archaic
character that is only understood by antiquaries, and
are usually very badly done. In the list given, from the
best examples that could be obtained, it will be seen that
the first, second, fifth and sixth, which should be alike in all, vary
considerably; "four mark" seals are also given which show similar
variations.

萬曆六年辛巳製　年製　年造　大明時憲　大明

年製　年造　大明時憲年製　丁亥

Dates are also written thus: *Wan-leih pah nëen che.*
Wan-löih eighth year, made 1580.

All these may be known as dates by the last characters,
Nëen year; and *che*, to make, form or fashion.

Sometimes another character is used, *Nëen tsaou*, made
or make.

Ta Ming-she-hëen, made in the time of the Great Ming
government. An example was found that probably read
thus: but it was too confused to be read with certainty;
the piece was modern ware.

Ta Ming nëen che, made in the years of the Great Ming.
This is also to be found, but is probably a modern mark.

Another mode of dating is by the cycle of sixty years,
but as only the year of the cycle is given it does not
identify the period.

24th year ... ... p blue

辛丑

子丑寅卯辰巳午未申酉戌亥 ｜ 甲乙丙丁戊己庚辛壬癸

38th year ... ... p red

The first column is called the ten celestial stems, and the second the twelve terrestial branches. The first year of the cycle is marked by the first character in each column, and they are used in regular order—the eleventh year being marked by the first "stem" and the eleventh "branch;" the thirteenth, by the third stem and the first branch, and so on in rotation, making a separate combination for the sixty years, till the first two come round again on the sixty-first.

The twelve "branches" are the Chinese Zodiac.

The Rat, Bull, Tiger, Rabbit, Dragon, Serpent, Horse Sheep, Monkey, Cook, Dog and Boar.

The ten "stems" are double characters; they are allied to the five Chinese elements: Water, Fire, Wood, Metal and Earth. This system is also used in Japan and Siam.

The 76th cycle commenced in 1864.

戊辰
年製

同治十二年 癸酉

明 大洪建永洪
武文樂熙

One example was written thus—

   Woo shin nëen che, 5th year   ...   p blue

An example has just been found where the date is given both by the year of the Emperor, and the year of the cycle.

T'hung-che shĭh urh nëen. Kwei yew, 12th year of Shung-che. 10th year of cycle=1874. The 11th year also commences in 1874.

DATES.

TA MING Dynasty		
Hung-woo ... 1368	宣正景天成	Seuen-te ... 1426
Kĕen-wăn ... 1399	德統泰順化	* Ching-t'hung 1436
Yung-lo ... 1403		King-tae ... 1450
Hung-he ... 1425		* T'hëen-shun 1457
		Ching-hwa ... 1465

   * *Some authorities reverse these two periods—they both belong to the Emperor Yung Ching, who was taken prisoner by the Tartars, and held captive for seven years.*

		Hung-che	...	1488
治 弘		Ching-tĭh	...	1506
德 正		Kea-tsing	...	1522
靖 嘉		Lung-king	...	1567
慶 隆		Wan-leĭh	...	1573
歷 萬		Tae-chang	...	1620
昌 泰		T'hëen-k'he	...	1621
啓 天		Tsung-ching	...	1628
禎 崇		Tsung-kwang		1644
光 弘		Shaou-woo	...	1646
武 紹		Lung-woo	...	1646
武 隆		Yung-leĭh	...	1647
曆 永				

靖 大	TA TH'SING Dynasty			
命 天	—			
聰 天	T'hëen-ming	...	1616
德 崇	T'heen-tsing	...	1627
始 順	Tsung-te	...	1636
熙 康	Shun-che	...	1644
正 雍	Kang-he	...	1662
隆 乾	Yung-ching	...	1723
慶 嘉	Këen-lung	...	1736
光 道	Kea-king	...	1796
豐 咸	Taou-kwang	...	1822
治 同	Han-fung	...	1851
	T'hung-she	...	1861

DATES in the "Seal" Character.

Six Characters.

Ta-th'sing, Shun-che nëen che 1644

	Kang-he ... 1662	
	Yung-ching 1723	
	Këen-lung ... 1736	
	Kea-king ... 1796	
	Taou-kwang 1822	
	Han-fung ... 1851	

T'hung-che ... 1861

Four Characters.

Ching-hwa ... 1465
  Probably a forgery.

Shun-che ... 1644

Këen-lung ... 1736

Taou-kwang 1822

Han-fung ... 1851

T'hung-che ... 1861

Two Characters.—
Name only.

T'hung-che ... 1861

DRAGON,

With five claws, is an Imperial emblem, with four, of the blood royal, and with three, of the nobility. *Lung-fung*, a dragon and a phœnix (divine bird of felicitous omen), was a mark of the *Seuen-te* period, 1426 to 1435.

FISH.

The two fish is a mark usually found on old blue or Nankin ware; it is one of the earliest known, from 969 to 1106. Cups with handles in the form of a red fish are of the *Seuen-te* period.

———

FLOWER.

Many varieties of this mark are found in blue and also in colours. A sesamum flower painted under the foot of a vase, &c., is a mark of *Tou-cheou*, 969 to 1106.

H

(*) Emblem of longevity.

Hoa, a small flower painted inside a cup, is a mark of the *Yung-lo* period, 1403 to 1424. It signifies pleasure in a vicious sense.

————

FLY,

Or Butterfly, is found on old "Nankin."

GRASS.

The "grass mark" is probably a water plant. About A.D. 960 some such mark was used to denote ware of the best quality.

INSCRIPTIONS.

A great variety are to be met with on old porcelain, often in the place where the European mark is found. Some are compliments and good wishes; others are in praise of the articles inscribed; many are quotations from the poets and classical authors of all ages. These last are not examplified.

Tsew, wine. Small white cups thus marked were used by the Emperor *Kea-tsing*, 1522 to 1566.

Këen, rectitude. Mark of an early period, said to be on articles sent to disgraced Mandarins.

Show, long life. This is a common Oriental compliment, "May you live for ever," and occurs oftener than any other character. It has many variations; sometimes a piece of pottery or porcelain is marked with a hundred or more; these are called "the hundred *show*."

Forms of *Show.*

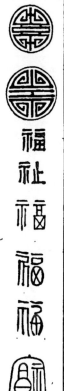

Show, is also drawn in circular, oval and elongated forms, thus :

Füh che or	}	Happiness, divine protection, felicity.
Che füh		
Füh che	,,	,,
,,	,,	,,
,,	,,	,,
,,	,,	,,

祿	*Lüh*	Wealth, great possessions.
綠	,,	{ *Show füh* and *lüh* are often found together.
吉	*Keih*	Felicity, good luck.
玉	*Yüh*	{ A gem, beautiful, precious, valuable, &c., Known as the F mark, being often indistinct, and like that letter.
文	*Wan*	{ Literature. On articles made for use of literary men, the ruling class of China.
興	*Hing*	Flourishing, highly esteemed.
囍	(?) *Ke*	A vessel, vase, ability, capacity.
囍	,,	,, ,,
寶	*Paou*	Precious, valuable.
廷	*Ting*	Perfect.

全	*Tsuen*	Perfect, a name.
慶	*King*	Good, excellent, congratulations.
汉	*Ch'ha*	Name.
五福	*Woo füh*	The five blessings: which are long life, riches, health, the love of virtue, and a natural death.
珎珍	*Woo chin*	The five precious things, as above. This is an example of the way the marks are usually written.
珍玉	*Chin yüh*	Precious or valuable gem.
玉珍	*Yüh chin*	Gem of great value; pearl of great price.
玩玉	*Wan yüh*	Delightful gem or beautiful jewel.

珍玩	*Chin wan*	A valuable curiosity.
大吉	*Ta keïh*	{ Great prosperity, felicity or good fortune.
樞府	*Choo foo*	{ A pivot, and the most polite expression for the house of another. Palace of the centre of the universe—mark used 1260–1367.
薑湯	*Keang t'ang*	Ginger preserved in syrup.
棗湯	*Tsaou t'ang*	{ A fruit (called dates, by Europeas) in syrup—*Chow Chow*. Both marks of the *Kea-tsing* period, 1522–66.
同安	*Tung gan*	Name—imp on old ware.
永盛	*Yung ching*	Name—p blue ,,

爲玞乘	*Wei foo ching*	{ Made to multiply (or increase the stock of) veined jasper.
仁和館	*Jin ho kwan*	Hall of brotherhood and peace.
奉先堂	*Fung seen tang*	{ Hall for the honourable reception of those who have gone before. Hall of ancestors.
堂奇 製玉	*Khe yŭh* *tang che*	} Hall of wonderful beauty, made (for)
堂彩 製閏	*Tsae jun* *tang che*	} Brilliantly adorned Intercalary hall, made.

堂製偵德	*Ching tih* *tang che*	} Hall of virtuous research, made.
堂製珮玉	*Pei yŭh* *tang che*	} Hall of the jewelled girdle, made.
堂製紫刺	*Tze tze* *tang che*	} Hall of the violet embroidery, made.
堂製敬畏	*King wei* *tang che.*	} Hall of worship and veneration, made.
即佛日㲉	*Ming* *Fuh* *Yuě* *Tang*	} The illustrious Fo's (or Buddha) hall of audience or prayer.

佳 玉 罢 堂	*Yŭh tang* *kea ke*	Beautiful vase (or excellent vessel) for the hall of gems—the Academy.
長 富 春 貴	*Fŭh kwei* *chang chun*	Wealth, honours, and a long spring time, or lasting youth.
長 富 命 貴	*Fŭh kwei* *chang ming*	Wealth, honours and long life.
賜 天 福 官	*Tĕen kwan* *tsze fŭh*	May heaven confer happiness.
如 奇 五 珍	*Khe chin* *jou wou*	Wonderful as the five precious things.
如 奇 玉 珍	*Khe chin* *jou yŭh*	Wonderful precious-stone resembling a jewel.

奇玩 如玉	*Khe wan* *jou yŭh*	Wonderful precious stone, resembling a jewel.
聖友 雅集	*Ching yew* *ya tseïh*	Remarkable meeting of philosophers and friends.
博古 珍玩	*Pŏ koo* *chin wan*	For the learned in antiquities, a valuable curiosity.
文玉 宝鼎	*Wan yŭh* *paou ting*	Elegant, perfect and precious, *ting* or metal vase used for burning joss stick or incense.
文章 山斗	*Wan shang* *Shan tow*	Literary essay. Compliment comparing the recipient to the mountain *Tae Shan* and the north pole or star, *Pih tow.*
美玉 雅製	*Mei yŭh* *ya che*	Made for the connoisseur of beautiful gems.

萬疆壽 無彊壽 *Wan show* *woo keang*	} An unlimited long life.
萬壽彌蝉 *Wan* *Show* *Woo* *Keang*	} „ „ In "Seal" character.
皇江呢 造萬明 *Keang ming* *kaou tsaou*	} *Keang ming kaou* maker.
祥萬明 製明 *Wan ming* *chiang che*	} *Wan ming chiang* made it.

雍正 御製	Yung ching yu che	} Made for the service of *Yung ching*.
連成 奇后	Lëen ching khe how	} (?) Name.
若深 珍藏	Jo shin chin tsang	Name. Precious property.
	"	} This mark is of frequent occurrence, but is usually very indistinct.
	"	
奇石寶 鼎之珍	Khe she paou ting che chin	} Ting, or incense burner, of valuable and extraordinary precious stone.

奇玉宝　忠有美　壽比南山
鼎之珍　玉雅製　福如東海

Khe yŭh paou ⎱
ting che chin ⎰ Ting, or incense burner, of valuable and extraordinary precious stone.

Chung yeu mei ⎱
yŭh ya che ⎰ For the possessor of a true and faithful heart this elegant gem was made.

Show pe nan shan, Long life as south mountain.

Foŭ jou tung hai, Happiness similar east sea.

Nan-shan is a mountain in *Fong-thesang-fou*. The inscription may be read, May you live to be as old as the hills, and your happiness be as great as the sea is wide.

———

KWEI,

or badge of authority, probably a seal of office; denotes that the piece was made for the use of a Mandarin; the four are often found together, but they also occur singly.

Wan-tse, Ten thousand things, everything, all creation. The "swastika" or fylfot; cross of Buddha.

　　　　　　"　　　　　　　　　　"

　　　　　　"　　　　　　　　　　"

Kwei.

"Sounding Stone" or gong.

This is also intended to give forth a sound when struck; it is used as a tuning fork; it has been mistaken for a Masonic emblem.

Pearl or Mandarin button.

　　　　　　"　　　　　　　　　　"

Kwei, or sceptre of stone, and musical instruments.

LEAF.

The leaf mark is very common on pieces of every period; there is no certain information to be had about it.

(?) Bamboo leaves; used as a mark in a factory of King-te-chin, 1573 to 1619.

,,　　　　　,,

			NUMERALS.				
壹	一	丨	Yĭh ...	...	...	...	1
貳	二	刂	Urh ...	...	...	...	2
叄	三	川	San ...	...	...	...	3
肆	四	ㄨ	Sze ...	...	...	...	4
伍	五	ㄡ	Woo	...	...	...	5
陸	六	乚	Lew ...	...	...	...	6
柒	七	亠	Tseïh	...	...	...	7
捌	八	亖	Pă ...	...	...	...	8
玖	九	夂	Kew	...	...	...	9
拾	十	卄	Shĭh...	...	...	...	10

These are given to assist in deciphering dates.

PRECIOUS THINGS.

Instruments used by the *literati*; a stone for grinding the ink, brushes for writing, and a roll of paper; early mark.

Precious Things.

———

RABBIT,

or Hare, found on old Nankin ware.

———

SACRED AXE,

on pieces made for warriors.

———

SHELL,

or Helmet, probably for same.

———

SQUARE.

Paou. Precious, valuable.

Kwo, a nation or people. (?) Name.

 Te shan, name.

 Shan‾yŭh, name.

 On old ware, dragon pattern.

    ,,   ,,

 Found on old Nankin ware; imitated by factories of Europe.

 Maker or decorator's mark. Called House marks by the Chinese.

    ,,   ,,

    ,,   ,,

Maker or Decorator's mark.

Foŭ kwei } Beautiful vase for the wealthy and
kea ke or }   noble; or wealth, honours, and a vast
wong ke }   intellect or capacity.

(?) *how* }
         } Probably name.
choo she }

Chin chow }
         } Valuable (vase) to explain the future.
she tsuen }

Examples of marks on Canton ware of recent date, possibly to represent the Imperial "seal."

     ,,   ,,   ,,

     ,,   ,   ,,

Examples of marks on Canton ware, of recent date, possibly to represent the Imperial " Seal."

,,   ,,   ,,   .

,,   ,   ,,

———

TABLE.

Many varieties of this mark are found on old Nankin ware. It was imitated by Delft, Dresden, Worcester, and other factories of Europe.

These figures occur so often on old ware, especially that intended for sacrificial use, that a few words may be given to explain their purport.

The unbroken line *Yang*, represents the masculine or perfection; the divided line *Yin*, the feminine or imperfection. The group of four is called the *Sze-seang* or four similitudes; the eight are the *Pa-qua* or eight symbols of *Fŏh-he*. The circle was added by *Chow*, a member of the *Sung* dynasty, who analysed and explained them.

The circle represents the original principle, the waved line dividing it makes the dual power or the active and passive principles of creation, it is called the *Tae-keih*, this when in action, produced a male power, when at rest a female power. From these were generated four visible forms which represent in the innumerable combinations of the eight symbols, the changes and transmutations that take place in nature and in the affairs of the world.

JAPAN.

THE manufacture of porcelain is said to date from 27 B.C. It was greatly improved in the beginning of the thirteenth century by a Japanese potter, who visited *King-te-chin* and other factories of China in the disguise of a priest. The pottery of Japan is of still greater antiquity, and pieces are still in existence that are said to be 3000 years old. The old ware is highly valued, and the small wine cups, called *Soma* cups, are only used on special occasions. They are a dark-coloured crackle ware, decorated with running horses and marked at the side with the badge of *Soma*, eight dots round a central ninth.

The great centre of the Japanese manufacture is in the province of *Hezen*, where twenty-five villages are congregated on a mountain which affords a plentiful supply of material for their work. Other districts have, however, their peculiar wares, some of which are undoubtedly of great antiquity.

The marks used in Japan are usually the name of the factory or of the maker or decorator; sometimes all are given.

DATES

are written in the Chinese manner, the name of the Japanese period being used. The only examples that vary in any way from those already given under "China," are:

Ten-show, 7th year ...　　　...　　　... 1579

Show-o, 2nd year ...　　　...　　　... 1653

DATES.

德建	Ken-tok	1370	正康	Kō-show ...	1455
中文	Bun-tin	1372	祿長	Chiyo-rok ...	1457
授天	Ten-du	1375	正寛	Kwan-show ...	1460
和弘	Ko-wa	1380	正文	Bun-show ...	1466
中元	Gen-tin	1380	仁應	Ō-nin	1467
四明	Mei-tok the IV.	1393	明文	Bun-mei ...	1469
永應	Ō-yei	1394	亨長	Tiyo-kiyo ...	1487
長正	Show-tiyo ...	1428	德延	En-tok	1489
享永	Yei-kiyo	1429	應明	Mei-ō	1492
吉嘉	Ka-kitsu ...	1441	龜文	Bun-ki	1501
安文	Bun-an	1444	正永	Yei-show ...	1504
德宝	Ho-tok	1449	永大	Dai-jei	1521
德亭	Kiyo-tok ...	1452	祿亭	Kiyo-rok ...	1528

Di-yei	1532	Yen-pō	1673
Ko-dai	1555	Ten-wa	1681
Yei-rok	1558	Tei-kiyo... ...	1684
Gen-ki	1570	Gen-rok	1688
Ten-show ...	1573	Ho-yei	1704
Bun-rok	1592	Show-tok ...	1711
Kei-chiyo ...	1596	Kiyo-ho	1717
Gen-wa	1615	Gen-bun	1736
Kwan-jei ...	1624	Kwan-pō ...	1741
Show-ho	1644	Yen-kiyo ...	1744
Kei-an	1648	Kwan-jen ...	1748
Show-ō	1652	Ho-reki	1751
Mei-reki	1655	Mei-wa	1764
Man-dai	1658	An-jei	1772
Kwan-bun ...	1661	Ten-mei	1781

	Kwan-sei	...	1789		久	文	An-sei	...	...	1854
政	寛	Kiyo-wa	...	...	1801	治	元	Man-yen	...	1860
和	享	Bun-kwa	...	1804	應	慶	Bun-kin	...	...	1861
化	文	Bun-sei	...	...	1818	治	明	Gen-di	...	...	1861
政	文	Ten-pō	...	...	1834	政	安	Kei-ō	...	...	1865
保	天	Ko-kua	...	...	1844	延	萬	Mei-di	...	...	1868
化	弘	Ka-yei	...	...	1848					
永	嘉								

ENAMEL.

Cloisonné enamel on porcelain is peculiar to Japan, and but few specimens have reached Europe, it is exquisitely fine, the flat wire with which the pattern is formed, not being thicker than a hair and less than the 32nd of an inch in depth.

The porcelain is thick and decorated with blue; it is difficult to ascertain the age of the specimens imported; they seldom bear a mark.

山
半   *Yama-han*, Name.

Ching-hwa   ...   ...   p blue

nëen che, Chinese date 1645–1687; probably a forgery.

Di-Ni-pon, Great Japan.

Han-suki sae, Han-suki, maker   p blue

Pottery is also enamelled in the same way; some examples of *Ki-yòto* ware marked *kin-kou-san*, have lately been imported.

Ni-pon Si-to, Japan Sito.

(illegible) *Eu-rock sae, Eurok* maker   p blue

FACTORIES.

Arranged as known in England except when marked with name of place where made.

AWATA. Pottery of fine quality with a delicate crackled glaze, cream or vellum colour, decorated with painting in enamel colours, and sometimes gold. Probably *Kiyo-to*. *Awa-ta.*

Dio-to, maker ... ... imp black

Di Ni-pon, Great Japan.

Dio-to sae, Dioto maker ... p blue

To-kio, Place
Mats-moto
Yashi-nobo, name ... ... p red
    Both marks on same piece

Ae-rako, name ... ... imp

Ki-yo, name ... ... ,,

Yu-ah-su-zan, name ... ... ,,

Hira-do Mika-wa outchi.

Hira-do of   „   ...   p red

HEZEN or HESHU. Porcelain of fine quality and egg shell ware, decorated with colour; also blue, in imitation of Nankin ware or ornamented with flowers modelled in slight relief.

He-zen, sometimes called Fi-zen.

He-shu.

He-zen.

Hari-ta-ka-mi, name.

He-zen.

Shin-po dzo, maker   ...   ...   p red

从碟山 仍而造	*Hezen.*
	Rek-sen dzo, maker.
西肥有田山	*Nisi Hezen hari-da-yama,* West Hezen. Name of factory.
南里製	*Nan-di sae,* maker ... ... p red
肥州有田	
石太造	*He-shu. Hari-dan,* factory.
	Ten-tai dzo. Ten-tai, maker ... p blue
	Villages of HEZEN, occupied by potters.
	The first two factories do not make ware for sale.
山内河大	*Oo kavatsi yama,* Great mountain between rivers.
山内河三	*Mi kavatsi yama,* Three mountains between rivers.
山泉和	*Idsoumi yama,* Mountain of the springs.
平髙攵	*Kan ko fira,* Beautiful upper plain.
平野本	*Fon ko fira,* Beautiful principal plain.
平野中	*Naka no fira,* Middle plain,

I

平長 郎大 郎中 川白 町亦 屋岩 剏南 尾圕 田モ黒 獺廣 獺ノ一 左井	*Naga fira,* Long or large plain. *Oo tarou,* Great vase. *Naka tarou,* Middle (sized) vase. *Sira kava,* White brook or clear spring. *Akaye matsi,* Street of the painters in red. *I vaya,* The cave. *Minami kawara,* South bank (of river). *Hoka o,* Outside tail. *Kuro mouda,* Black field. *Firo se,* Blue porcelain made here. *Itche-na-se.* *Imali,* Fine transparent porcelain made here.

KAGA or KUTANI.

Pottery and coarse porcelain usually decorated with elaborate paintings in red and gold, sometimes blue or green is introduced.

Ku-tani, the nine valleys. Name of the place where the factories of the Prince of Kaga are situated. p red.

九谷

Ku-tani		p gold on red
,, ...		,,
Ku-tani tzo, made at Kutani ...		,,
,, ,, ...		p red
Ka-gayo *Ku-tani* } K. in Kaga ...		... p gold
,, ,,		
,, ,, ...		... p. red
,, ,, *dzo*, made ...		... p black

九穀
九谷造
九谷 卯陽
九谷 加湯
加天九為米

Di Ni-pon, great Japan	
Ku-tani sae, made at K.	p black
Ku-tani Bok-zan (name) ... ... mountain of the trees.	p blue
Ku-tani, on either side of name *Tou-zan* ...	p red
Tou-zan, Porcelain mountain (name) ...	p red
Kiyohu-zan, Mountain of the rising sun (name)	p red
Pon-zan, place	imp
Dio-tzo, maker, on same piece with *kutani* mark	,,

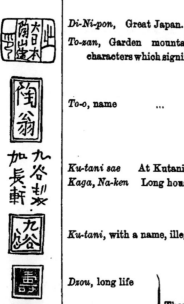

Di-Ni-pon, Great Japan.

To-zan, Garden mountain (name). On either side characters which signify, Strong pottery. p red

To-o, name ... ... p red

Ku-tani sae At Kutani made.
Kaga, Na-ken Long house, factory ... p black

Ku-tani, with a name, illegible ... p gold on red

Dzou, long life

Fou-kou, happiness

Rau-kou, riches

These characters are often found on *Kaga* ware, singly, together, and both with and without factor marks.

京都

KIYOTO or KIOTO.

Same as "Awata," and often called "Satsma" ware.

Kiyo-to ...   . p red

錦老山造 日本京都

Ni-pon Kiyo-to, Japan, Kiyoto.

Kin-kou-zan tzo (name) maker   ... p gold

錦老

Kin-kou-zan (name)...   ...   ... imp on same
pieces

SATSMA or SATSUMA.

Pottery, often of coarse quality, with delicate crackle
glaze; finely pencilled decoration in gold, with a little
color.   No marks known on undoubted old ware.

Itsi-gaya, name of place in Satsma.

Tai-zan, maker's name   ...   ... imp

Tai-zan   ., ... ,,

帶 山 帶
山 山

田
香

車 卯 芝 住
生 月 雲 亭
六 ┃ 住
13 臺 亭
九 肆 青 柔
雲 郤 芝 住
房 臺 雲
九 亭
住

Tai-zan, name ... ... „

„ „ ... ... p black

Den-ko, name ... ... imp

SHIBA in Tokei.

Pottery painted in enamel colours, of good quality, called
Awata ware.

Resident of *Shiba* in *Tokei.*

Sei-un-tei, name of factory.

Hikomaro, maker's name ... ... p black

„ ... ... p blue

An old mark, date unknown.

OWARI, or AWARI.

Small ware of fine porcelain, decorated in blue, colours and gold, often painted at *Tokio*.

Owari.

Saeng-ets, beautiful moon; name of a celebrated painter on porcelain.

Ai-we, name ,, ,,

Sin-zad foudi, spring mountain (name), painter.

,, ,, p black

Yama-moto Sho-tan, name of well known painter.

FLOWER.

Many varieties of this mark occur on porcelain both old and of recent date.

LEAF.

And other varieties are often found on porcelain.

INSCRIPTIONS

Of a similar character to the Chinese are found on all kinds of ware.

Dsou, long life.

   ,,   for variations see the hundred *show* in the Chinese inscriptions.

Foukou, happiness.

Raukou, wealth.

So-o, name	... ...	h p	imp
Kami sae, Kami, maker ...	...	,,	p blue
Rakou-maza dzo ,, ,, maker.	... ...	,,	p red
Huzi-nori, name	... ...	,,	p blue
Jo-shin } name ... *Chin tsang* } precious property An imitation of an old Chinese mark.	...	,, ,,	,, ,,
Shin fo *se-seki* } name		,,	,,
H'atsi fou *kie sha* { Assembly of the seven honorable societies. Mark of the Govern- ment works also found on enamelled ware		,,	,,

晉靜	唫舘	*Sin sits king kang*	}	Hall of the increase of peace and harmony	,,	p blue
富貴	長春	*Fou kwei chiwe sin*	}	Wealth, honours and a lasting youth.		
富貴	長命	*Fou kwei chwe min*	}	wealth, honours and long life.		
冨蚤	長命	,,	,, ,, ,,			
陶玉	圍製	*To gucou] eng sae]*	}	Made at the pottery of the beautiful garden	h p	p blue
陶玉圍	五耿制坟	*To gucou eng Gos ki sae]*	}	Same with makers name	,,	,,

Number 194 p red on blue ware, probably Hezen ; other pieces bore different numbers.

The Chinese dates *Seuen-tȟh* and

Ching-hwa are often found on Hezen ware decorated with old Nankin patterns.

Di *ni-pon*   } Great Japan.
Hi-rak dzo   } Hirak, maker   pot & h p

Tho xing ti } Pavilion of the spring time.
Tsi-tse tzo. } *Tsi tse*, maker   p red

Tho wing ti } Pavilion of the spring time.

San-fo tzo } *San fo*, maker ... p red

Both on *Nakasaki* ware.

Ni-pon Si-to, Japan, Sito, name of place.

Kama-moto mosa-kitchi tzo

   ,,   ,,   maker ...   ,,
 This was also on *Nagasaki* ware; an enamelled vase is also marked *Sito*.

SQUARE.
Called House Marks.

Hata, Name of a factory ... h p   p red

San-han, mountain middle, name ...   ,,   p blue

Yeh-san or } one mountain, name   ,,   ,,
Itsi-yama }

Goa, strong, name ...   ... h p   p blue

All on blue decorated ware called *Hezen;* marks such as these are found in great variety, they often differ in a set of cups and saucers that are evidently from the same hand.

This appears to be " happiness."

Probably an emblem of longevity.

———

VASE.

This curious mark is impressed and coloured; it represents a sacred vessel used in sacrificing and is inscribed with the characters *Foukou*, happiness, and *dzou*, longevity.

W. H. H.

Lightning Source UK Ltd.
Milton Keynes UK
20 February 2011
167858UK00001B/6/P